Richard G. Beau

D0446839

Australian Cattle Dogs

Everything about Purchase, Care,
Nutrition, Breeding, Behavior, and Training

With 49 Photographs

Drawings by Michele Earle-Bridges

BARRON'S

Acknowledgments

The author wishes to acknowledge the assistance of Norman and Carolyn Herbel and Marge Blankenship for their assistance in making this project a reality. Their knowledge of the breed and dedication to maintaining the true character and working ability of the Australian cattle dog provided the inspiration and basis for my research.

© Copyright 1997 by Barron's Educational Series, Inc.

All rights reserved.

No part of this book may be reproduced in any form by photostat, microfilm, xerography, or any other means, or incorporated into any information retrieval system, electronic or mechanical, without the written permission of the copyright owner.

All inquiries should be addressed to:
Barron's Educational Series, Inc.
250 Wireless Boulevard
Hauppauge, NY 11788

International Standard Book No. 0-8120-9854-4

Library of Congress Catalog Card No. 96-29857

Library of Congress Cataloging-in-Publication Data
Beauchamp, Richard G.
  Australian cattle dog : everything about purchase, care, nutrition, breeding, behavior, and training / Richard G. Beauchamp ; drawings by Michele Earle-Bridges.
       p.   cm. — (A complete pet owner's manual)
  Includes bibliographical references (p.   ) and index.
  ISBN 0-8120-9854-4
  1. Australian cattle dog. I. Title. II. Series.
SF429.A77B43   1997
636.737—dc21
                                    96-29857
                                        CIP

Printed in China

19 18 17 16 15 14 13 12 11

About the Author

Richard G. Beauchamp has been a lifelong dog breeder and exhibitor. He has judged all breeds of purebred dogs in every major country of the world and written about dogs and dog breeding for publications in many countries including Australia, England, and America. He has observed the Australian cattle dog at work on the huge ranches in the breed's homeland and has also visited organizations in Australia that have been officially entrusted with the protection of the dingo as a native animal.

Photo Credits

Cabal Canine Candids: front cover, contents page top, contents page bottom, pages 8, 29 bottom left; Paulette Braun: inside front cover, pages 17 bottom, 25 top, 33 top right, 36, 61, 65, 89, 92; Marge Blankenship: inside back cover, pages 21 top right, 25 bottom, 32, 88; Susan Green: back cover, pages 9, 20 left, 20 right, 21 top left, 21 bottom, 24, 28 top, 28 bottom, 29 top, 33 top left, 40, 60, 76, 80; Jayne Langdon: pages 7, 73; Lori Herbel: page 13; Jean Wentworth: pages 16, 44 bottom, 93; Fox & Cook Photography: pages 17 top, 72 top; Wm. Kohler & Associates: pages 29 bottom right, 44 top; Toni Tucker: pages 45, 69; Sandy Arborgast: page 64; Courtesy of Carol Anne Kriesel: page 49; Courtesy of Marge Blankenship: page 72 bottom.

Important Notes

This pet owner's guide tells the reader how to buy and care for an Australian cattle dog. The author and the publisher consider it important to point out that the advice given in the book is meant primarily for normally developed puppies from a good breeder—that is, dogs of excellent physical health and good character.

Anyone who adopts a fully grown dog should be aware that the animal has already formed its basic impressions of human beings. The new owner should watch the animal carefully, including its behavior toward humans, and should meet the previous owner. If the dog comes from a shelter, it may be possible to get some information on the dog's background and peculiarities there. There are dogs that, as a result of bad experiences with humans, behave in an unnatural manner or may even bite. Only people that have experience with dogs should take in such animals.

Caution is further advised in the association of children with dogs, in meeting with other dogs, and in exercising the dog without a leash.

Even well-behaved and carefully supervised dogs sometimes do damage to someone else's property or cause accidents. It is therefore in the owner's interest to be adequately insured against such eventualities, and we strongly urge all dog owners to purchase a liability policy that covers their dog.

Contents

In 1840, Thomas Hall began experimenting with infusions of dingo blood to create the ideal cattle dog. Dingoes like this pup were crossed with imported smooth-coated collies.

Dingoes hand-reared by the aborigines produced a relatively tame dog that was easily taught to track and hunt. This young dingo is being obedience trained at the Merigal Dingo Education Centre in Sydney, Australia.

Preface

Upon hearing that I had accepted a judging assignment in Australia, my long-time friends Donn and Debbie Harling asked me if I had ever seen a litter of newborn Australian cattle dogs. The year was 1977 and at that time I had seen few adult cattle dogs much less new-born puppies.

The female they had with them in their motor home had whelped the day before, several days ahead of schedule and had given birth to a litter of six. On seeing them, I immediately remarked, "I had no idea the breed came in all white."

"They don't," was Donn's reply. "They're born white and don't develop their color until they're a few weeks old. Probably due to their Dalmatian heritage."

"Dalmatian?" I couldn't help but ask. I was fascinated.

"Yes, and it is said they have bull terrier and kelpie blood as well," Donn went on. "But the primary cross was collie and the Australian wild dingo."

This conversation ignited my fascination for the Australian cattle dog. On my trips to Australia in the following years I made it a special point to ask my Australian judging mentor, Dr. Harry Spira, to assist me in learning more about what was to me a "new" breed.

I traveled to several working cattle ranches with Dr. Spira and saw the Australian cattle dogs perform amazing feats of courage and proficiency with the huge, nearly wild cattle they were charged with. We also visited the Australian Native Dog Training Society and the Merigal Dingo Educa-tion Centre at Bargo, New South Wales. The organizations were under the supervision of Bernice Walters who was also breeder of the internationally famous line of Wooleston Australian cattle dogs.

With great fascination through the years I have followed the somewhat successful attempts of the members of the Australian Native Dog Training Society of New South Wales to domesticate the dingo. I have also come to appreciate the unique character and exceptional working ability of the well-bred Australian cattle dog. Acknowledging my interest in the Australian cattle dog and its heritage, Donn and Debbie Harling invited me to write the introduction to their classic work on the breed in America, *Australian Cattle Dogs, The First Five Years, 1980–1985*. I was delighted to accept and the book, the first devoted to the breed in America, was published in 1986.

There has been a dearth of literature on the Australian cattle dog in America, particularly regarding the breed as a companion and family member. I feel confident that *Australian Cattle Dogs: A Complete Pet Owner's Manual* will fill that gap. It will also assist those individuals contemplating the purchase of an Australian cattle dog by not only giving them some insight into the character of the breed but also into the necessary characteristics and temperament of the prospective owner.

Richard G. Beauchamp

History and Origin of the Australian Cattle Dog

"Horses for Courses"

"Horses for courses" is an old saying among British stockmen that has served as the basis for development of many kinds of prized livestock. Translated into layman's terms, this adage simply means choosing a formula that will produce a horse best suited to the terrain of the region in which the horse will work. This formula applied not only to horses but was the basis upon which many of Great Britain's outstanding livestock dogs were developed. This unique ability of the British was to be given its greatest test in the late eighteenth century.

When the early settlers from the United Kingdom began to migrate to Australia in the 1780s they took their livestock with them. Once in the new country they realized many of the tried-and-true rules governing animal husbandry they had learned in their homeland had to be readjusted to this new and rugged "land down under." The environment in which their livestock now lived differed dramatically and therefore the animals themselves behaved differently.

There were vast grazing lands available upon which the settlers could raise cattle and sheep. No longer confined by the space restrictions they had experienced in Great Britain, these immense land tracks encouraged stockmen to develop huge herds of not only sheep but also of the more space-needy cattle. While an economic boon, the large herds were to create problems for ranchers they had not earlier been called upon to deal with. Because the cattle roamed the outback, unsupervised and unconfined, they were at best half wild. The cattle were not only difficult to keep track of but treacherous to the human hands hired to work with them.

British cattlemen had long relied upon the assistance of their highly developed sheepdogs to maintain the placid sheep and cattle in their homeland. However, these same dogs that had proven so capable in Great Britain met conditions in Australia they were ill equipped to cope with.

The new Australians were met with a challenge that a people less experienced in animal husbandry might never have been able to meet. It was their long-practiced ability to develop "horses for courses" that saved the day and helped provide Australia with an economically successful cattle industry.

To help them deal with the myriad of problems their new homeland provided, the Australians developed an incomparable herding dog, a wonder dog so rugged, so uncannily intelligent, and so courageous that the breed was eventually to gain admiration and popularity throughout the entire world. This was the Australian cattle dog. The formula that produced this incomparable working dog is as fascinating as the breed itself. One must be familiar with the history of the Australian cattle dog in order to fully understand and appreciate the breed's unique nature and functional physique. The breed's story begins thousands of years before Western people had any knowledge that the island continent of Australia even existed.

The Dingo

Long before the first Europeans set foot on Australian shores there existed on that island continent a wolflike dog that the aboriginal population called *Worrigal* or dingo. It was first assumed the dingo had accompanied aboriginal people to Australia in their earliest migrations tens of thousands of years ago. Anthropological evidence has shown that aboriginal people have lived in Australia for at least 40,000–50,000 years; however, the irrefutable evidence of carbon dating actually places the oldest dingo fossil ever found at 3,450 years old. The mystery of how the dingo made its way to Australian shores has yet to be solved but there is no question that the dingo adapted to the rugged and varied Australian environment with great ease and enjoyed a pleasant coexistence with aboriginal man.

Research indicates the dingo is closely related to dogs that exist from Israel, east to Vietnam, north to the Himalayas, and southward through Indonesia, Borneo, and New Guinea. These all are descended from the Indian wolf rather than the northern timber wolf from which most other domestic dogs descend. It is theorized that semi-domesticated descendants of the Indian wolf accompanied the Indo-Malayan boat people in their migrations from Asia's mainland a little over 4,000 years ago and were used as barter and gifts.

The dogs that reached Australian shores evolved into what is known as the dingo, now afforded distinction as a separate subspecies of the domestic dog called *Canis familiaris dingo*. These dogs, which acclimated themselves to Australia, were never subjected to the same domestication pressures as the descendants of the northern timber wolf throughout Europe. Rather, they developed an independent yet close relationship with the aborigines. The dingo lived both in the aboriginal camps and in the wild. This simultaneous existence is documented by the writings of the earliest explorers who first tracked across the Australian continent.

The aborigines would take young dingoes from the nest, preferably before the pups' eyes were open, and would hand-feed or even suckle the youngsters. This human socialization process produced a relatively tame dog that was easily taught to track and hunt. The camp dogs were basically fed the same food their aboriginal owners ate. The dingoes that existed in the wild survived on a diet that consisted of the plentiful native game ranging in size from kangaroos to small rodents.

The first dingo and smooth-collie crosses produced a dog that worked silently and from the rear, snapping at the heels of the cattle when needed.

The Indo-Malayan semi-domesticated dogs that reached Australian shores over 4,000 years ago evolved into what is known as the dingo. Here a mother dingo nurses her pups.

Early written records describe dingo color as primarily shades of red. A few were black and tan or white. Pure dingoes were always seen to have a white tail tip and usually had white feet. The operative word here is "pure" in that dingoes readily mate with domestic dogs. Ticking or brindling of the white areas and piebald markings in the modern dingo are typical signs of crossbreeding with the domestic dog.

The Dingo as the Enemy of Humans

The dingo played an important role in the ecology of the land. It was a key figure in the checks and balances nature imposes and was respected for its role by the aborigines. The arrival of the vulnerable sheep herds in Australia provided a readily available diet alternative for the dingo. Its immediate addiction to sheep flesh quickly earned the dingo the reputation as a formidable enemy of pastoral people. The dingo was hunted and trapped

without mercy but even at that it proved to be a wily adversary, surviving the harshest measures imposed for its eradication.

It is interesting to note that since the early European settlers despised the dingo for the havoc it wreaked upon their herds, they were grudgingly forced to respect the animal. No true stockman could do otherwise, for here was a canny survivor that could more often than not outmaneuver humans. These humans could not help but be aware and appreciative of the dingo's many survival attributes.

The dingo's determination and courage in the hunt knew no bounds. Dingoes do not bark, and they were able to swiftly and silently dispatch their prey. Their tireless conformation and incredible constitutions enabled them to cope with the most inhospitable temperatures and environmental conditions.

The stockmen's attempts to eradicate this livestock enemy only resulted in proving how uncannily intelligent these wild canines were. It was because of their awareness of the dingo's many adaptive characteristics that the new Australians turned to the native dog when it came time to employ the "horses for courses" formula they had relied upon in their original homeland.

The First Australian Cattle Dogs

The sensible, hard-working, and devoted dogs that were first used to work cattle in Australia found it difficult to handle the country's torrid summer temperatures, rough terrain, and vast distances that needed to be traversed. This was not the British Isles-not by a long shot! On top of that, the dogs barked incessantly, keeping the drovers' horses on edge and the near-wild cattle in a constant state of nervous frenzy that worried the hard-won fat right off their bones.

Several herdsman, seeing many of the qualities that their own dogs lacked in the dingo, attempted crossing their own herding breeds with the Australian native dog. These early crosses proved unsatisfactory because of their extreme aggressiveness. Left to their own devices the offspring of these matings would attack and eat sheep and could not control young calves.

It was not until the year 1840 that a certain Thomas Hall, who lived about 150 miles south of Sydney in the state of New South Wales, imported a pair of blue merle smooth-coated highland collies. He was disappointed to learn that, while they were willing and able sheepherders, neither the original pair nor their progeny were able to handle the fractious cattle or the hostile environment. Hall began experimenting with infusions of dingo blood and even the first crosses produced a dog that gave great promise.

The progeny of these original crosses worked silently. Instead of charging at the head of the cattle as their sheep-oriented collie ancestors did, the dogs worked from the rear, snapping at the heels of the cattle when needed. Working from the rear kept the cattle moving forward rather than challenging the dogs when they were charged from the head.

This first generation cross resembled small, heavily made dingoes. They were either blue-mottled or red-speckled in color. Reports of the successful cross spread throughout New South Wales and the neighboring state of Queensland. The breed grew in demand as word of their cattle herding ability grew. There was only one drawback to these smooth collie and dingo crosses—they tended to treat the stockmen's horses much like the cattle. They would often snap at the heels of the horses in a misguided attempt to have them join the cattle. Thus, it

There are two colors permitted in Australian cattle dogs—blue and red speckle.

became obvious that any herding dog would have to have an amiable relationship with the drovers' horses.

A Dalmatian Cross

In due course Jack and Harry Bagust, who lived near Sydney, bred one of their best dingo and smooth collie-cross females to a Dalmatian that had recently been imported from Great Britain. Their thought was to improve their cattle dog's rapport with horses, a characteristic for which the Dalmatian was long known. The offspring from this cross were born white as all Dalmatians are but eventually developed blue speckle or red speckle coats at about three weeks.

The experiment was successful. The cross produced a dog that did in fact have a more workmanlike relationship with both horse and human. It is believed a bull terrier cross was made at this time as well, but unfortunately, the herding ability and herding desire of the offspring were significantly diminished. As a remedy breeders introduced the blood of the black and tan kelpie to the breeding program. The kelpies were a highly efficient Australian sheepdog. This produced a line of athletic dogs similar in type to the dingo but more muscular in build and distinctively colored.

The blue variety's body was dark blue, evenly speckled all over with a lighter blue. These dogs had black eye patches, black ears, and brown eyes. They also had tan legs, chests, and head markings. The red variety had dark red markings in place of black over an evenly speckled base.

Through selective breeding the dingo's athletic conformation and constitution, along with its intelligence and silent way of working, was maintained, as was the Dalmatian's devotion and protectiveness. This developing line of dogs was also heir to their sheepdog ancestor's ability to learn quickly and follow commands. The Australian stockmen had indeed developed

"horses for courses." The wonder dogs were particularly useful in the huge, sparsely settled cattle stations in northern New South Wales and the neighboring state of Queensland. In fact, the breed became so popular in Queensland that the dogs eventually took on the name of Queensland Heelers or Queensland Blue Heelers.

In 1893 Robert Kaleski, a highly respected Australian journalist and noted dog fancier, became avidly interested in this new breed and became its first chronicler. It is through his efforts that type and color were fixed. From Kaleski's pen came the first written standard of excellence firmly based upon the breed's dingo heritage. In 1902 this standard was submitted to and adopted by the Cattle and Sheep Dog Club of Australia and the Kennel Club of New South Wales. The newly accepted breed was officially given the name Australian cattle dog though to this day many proud owners in Australia refer to their dogs as Queensland Heelers or Queensland Blue Heelers.

The Breed Today

The Australian cattle dog has changed very little in the past century. While conformation and color have become more consistent throughout, breeders have been staunch in insisting that the intelligence and working ability of this breed should not be diminished. To this day it retains its superior herding ability and has become a devoted and protective home companion as well.

Armed with a definitive standard it is only logical that Aussie breeders began to look to the show ring with their breed that had already gained the admiration of any self-respecting stockman in the country. Australian cattle dogs were shown along with other station stock at the local agricultural shows.

Many breeds of dogs were used to create the Australian cattle dog. Pictured behind the Australian cattle dog, left to right, are the smooth-coated collie, Dalmatian, kelpie, dingo, and the bull terrier.

Original Australian Cattle Dog Standard
Authored by Robert Kaleski, Sydney, Australia, 1902

Head (15 points):	Broad between ears, tapering to a point at muzzle, full under the eye, strong and muscular in the jaws.
Ears (10 points):	Short and pricked, running to a point at tip; thick and set wide apart on the skull with plenty of muscle at the butts. Should be as decidedly pricked as a cat's.
Eyes (7 points):	Brown, quick and sly looking.
Shoulders (7 points):	Strong, with good slope for free action.
Chest (7 points):	Deep, but not out of proportion to body.
Legs (7 points):	Clean, fair amount of bone; very muscular.
Feet (7 points):	Small and cat shaped.
Back (7 points):	Straight, with ribs well sprung, ribbed up, and good loins; should arch slightly at loins.
Hindquarters (12 points):	Strong and muscular with back thighs well let down for speed; no dew claws on feet; tail, fair length "Dingo" or "bottle" shaped.
Height (7 points):	About 20 inches; bitches a little smaller.
Coat (7 points):	Short, smooth and very dense.
Colour (7 points):	Head, black or red; body, dark blue on back (sometimes with black saddle and black spot on tail butt.) Lighter blue sometimes mottled with white hairs on underpart of body; legs, bluish, with red spots mottled over them. Tail light blue, sometimes with white tip.
TOTAL: 100 points	
General Appearance:	That of a small thickset blue Dingo.
Faults:	Over/or under size, legginess, half pricked or lopping ears, overshot or undershot jaws; anything likely to diminish speed and endurance.

Usually, it was the rough-and-ready station owners who presented their dogs at the shows. Needless to say they and their dogs lacked the refinements developed in the less work-oriented breeds. While quality ran high, awards beyond the breed level were practically nonexistent; however, in the 1950s the breed made significant breakthroughs, particularly through the ring success of four dogs: Ch. Little Logic, his son Ch. Logic's Return, Ch. Trueblue Patches, and the all breed Best In Show winner, Ch. Hillside Duke.

The Australian Cattle Dog in the United States

People in the United States were not unaware of the merits of the Australian cattle dog; American ranchers from coast to coast had imported working stock and found the breed effective on their side of the Pacific.

A turning point for the breed in America came in 1967 when Christina Risk and Esther Ekman met at a dog show and decided to form a club dedicated to the advancement of the Australian cattle dog as a dual purpose dog-working dog and show dog.

The Australian cattle dog has become a favorite at dog shows.

The name of the club they organized was The Queensland Heeler Club of America, a name popularly used throughout Australia and by many Americans who owned the working cattle dogs. On the advice of the American Kennel Club, however, the name of the club was changed to the Australian Cattle Dog Club of America and ground work for recognition of the breed by the AKC was outlined. Christina Risk was named president of the club that was then made up of Australian cattle dog owners who kept their dogs expressly as working stock dogs.

It was at that time that the newly organized fanciers discovered that, of the twelve-strong membership, only two of the members could actually trace their dogs' ancestry back to dogs registered in Australia. A painful decision was made by the founding members who agreed that the only dogs that would be accepted into the registry of the club were those whose ancestry could be validated with paperwork to the Australian registry.

Fanciers Unite

Popularity of the breed grew slowly and steadily and fans were attracted from among exhibitors of other breeds. The working Australian cattle dog entered an entirely new phase of its existence in America—that of a show dog—but existing club members united and vowed never to forget the breed's working ability and they began to develop ways to encourage this desire on the part of newcomers.

Versatility Events
This was accomplished in part by including versatility events at all the Fun Matches held from 1978 on. The matches were held to comply with AKC requirements for breeds seeking AKC approval. The Versatility Program was developed to encourage the breed's working instinct and obedience trainability. The club was adamant that the Australian cattle dog would not become a mere "dog show statue."

The winner of the first ACDA Fun Match was Tallawong Blue Joshua who was bred by Helen Dickson and listed in the show results as owned by "Spicer."

An official standard of the breed based upon the existing Australian standard was drafted and approved by the AKC in 1979. The Australian cattle dog was granted official AKC recognition on May 1, 1980 and the first AKC shows at which the breed could be exhibited were held on September 1, 1980. In 1984 the Australian Cattle Dog Club of America held its first AKC-sanctioned specialty show and obedience trial. There were 183 entries and the regular classes were judged by Janet Wilcox. The sweepstakes classes were judged by Jimmie Brookings and obedience by Barbara Goodman. The versatility class of 22 was judged by Dawn O'Reilly.

Ch. Billabong The Lodestone was the winner of the first National specialty. He was bred by Lois K. Moody and owned by Lois Moody and Jean Raviola.

Official Standard for the Australian Cattle Dog
General appearance—The general appearance is that of a sturdy, compact, symmetrically built working dog.

This picture portrays an Australian cattle dog of the type called for in the AKC Breed Standard.

With the ability and willingness to carry out any task however arduous, its combination of substance, power, balance and hard muscular condition to be such that must convey the impression of a great agility, strength and endurance. Any tendency to grossness or weediness is a serious fault.

Characteristics—The utility purpose is assistance in the control of cattle, in both wide open and confined areas. Ever alert, extremely intelligent, watchful, courageous and trustworthy, with an implicit devotion to duty, making it an ideal dog. Its loyalty and protective instincts make a self-appointed guardian to the stockman, his herd, his property. Whilst suspicious of strangers, must be amenable to handling in the show ring.

Head—The head, in balance with other proportions of the dog, and in keeping with its general conformation, is broad of skull, and only slightly curved between the ears, flattening to a slight but definite stop. The cheeks are muscular, but not coarse nor prominent, the underjaw is strong, deep and well-developed. The foreface is broad and well filled in under the eye, tapering gradually to a medium length, deep and powerful muzzle. The lips are tight and clean. The nose is black irrespective of the color of the dog.

Teeth—The teeth should be sound, strong, and regularly spaced, gripping with a scissors-like action, the lower incisors close behind and just touching the upper. Not to be undershot nor overshot.

Eyes—The eyes should be oval shaped of medium size, neither prominent nor sunken, and must express alertness and intelligence. A warning or suspicious glint is characteristic. Eye color is dark brown.

Ears—The ears should be of moderate size, preferably small rather than large, broad at the base, muscular, pricked and moderately pointed (not spoon nor bat eared). Set wide apart on the skull, inclined outwards, sensitive in their use and firmly erect when alert. The inside of the ear should be fairly well furnished with hair.

Neck—The neck is of exceptional strength, muscular, and of medium length broadening to blend into the body and free from throatiness.

Forequarters—The shoulders are broad of blade, sloping, muscular and well angulated to the upper arm, and at the point of the withers should not be too closely set. The forelegs have strong round bone, extending to the feet without weakness at the pasterns. The forelegs should be perfectly straight viewed from the front, but the pasterns should show a slight angle with the forearm when regarded from the side.

Hindquarters—The hindquarters are broad, strong and muscular. The rump is rather long and sloping, thighs long, broad and well-developed, with moderate turn to stifle. The hocks are strong and well let down. When viewed from behind, the hind legs, from the hocks to the feet, are straight and placed neither close nor too wide apart.

Feet—The feet should be round and the toes short, strong, well-arched and held together. The pads hard and deep, and the nail must be short and strong.

Body—The length of the body from the point of the breast bone, in a straight line to the buttocks is greater than the height at the withers, as 10 is to 9. The topline is level, back strong, with ribs well sprung and ribbed back. (Not barrel ribbed.) The chest is deep and muscular, and moderately broad, loins are broad, deep and muscular with deep flanks strongly coupled between the fore and hindquarters.

Tail—The set on of the tail is low, following the contours of the sloping rump, and at rest should hang in a slight curve of a length to reach approximately to the hock. During movement and/or excitement it may be raised, but under no circumstances should any part of the tail be carried past a vertical line drawn through the root.

Coat—The weather resisting outer coat is moderately short, straight and medium texture, with short dense undercoat. Behind the quarters the coat is longer, forming a mild breeching. The tail is furnished sufficiently to form a good brush. The head, forelegs, hind legs from hock to ground, are coated with short hair.

Color (Blue)—The color should be blue or blue-mottled with or without other markings. The permissible markings are black, blue or tan markings on the head, evenly distributed for preference. The forelegs tan midway up the legs and extending up the front to the breast and throat, with tan on jaws: the hindquarters tan on inside of hind legs, and inside of thighs, showing down the front of the stifles and broadening out to the outside of the legs from hock to toes. Tan undercoat is permissible on the body providing it does not show through the blue outer coat. Black markings on the body are not desirable.

Color (Red Speckle)—The color should be a good even red speckle all over including the undercoat (not white or cream) with or without darker red markings on the head. Even head markings are desirable. Red markings on the body are permissible but not desirable.

Size—The desirable height at the withers to be within the following dimensions:

Dogs	18 to 20 inches
Bitches	17 to 19 inches

Dogs or bitches over or under these specified sizes are undesirable.

Movement—Soundness is of paramount importance. The action is true, free, supple and tireless, the movement of the shoulders and forelegs with the powerful thrust of the hindquarters, in unison. Capability of quick and sudden movement is essential. Stiltiness, loaded or slack shoulders, straight shoulder placement, weakness at elbows, pastern or feet, straight stifles, cow or bow hocks, must be regarded as serious faults.

Approved June 12, 1979

Understanding Australian Cattle Dogs

People find Australian cattle dogs attractive for various reasons. Though the breed can hardly be described as "pretty," many find the breed's simple, natural lines very handsome. Others are attracted to the Australian cattle dog's legendary intelligence and ability to understand its owner. While these are but a few of the valid assets of the Australian cattle dog, they are still not enough reason for anyone to rush out to buy an Australian cattle dog.

This is not a breed that can be put outdoors in a pen and attended to only when the owner has the time or notion to do so. It is a breed that is capable of becoming a great companion and cherished friend, but only if the owner is ready to invest the necessary time and patience in the training that is required to help the breed achieve its full potential.

Puppies spend most of their day investigating, digging, chewing, eating, and relieving themselves. This all takes a great commitment on the part of an owner.

As one devoted Australian cattle dog owner put it, "Lots of people *think* they want an Australian cattle dog, but if they knew more about the needs of the breed, they wouldn't. Some breeds are said to constantly be one step ahead of their owners; Australian cattle dogs stay at least *three* steps ahead!"

All puppies are cuddly and cute and may even spend a part of their day duplicating all those popular and appealing greeting card and calendar poses; however, it is important to realize that a puppy will spend only a very small part of its day in such a docile state. The far greater part of the day and night the puppy will spend investigating, digging, chewing, eating, relieving itself, needing to go outdoors, and then immediately insisting that it be let in. All too often these needs are not realistically considered before adding a dog to one's household.

The list of the real needs of a young puppy or an adult dog can be staggering to the uninitiated, and it takes a very concerned and dedicated owner to fulfill these needs, to say nothing of the time required for the many lessons an Australian cattle dog must be taught by its master before it understands what it may and may not do.

Friends often seek our advice when they are contemplating the purchase of their first dog. If we detect even the slightest uncertainty on their part, we always advise them to wait until they are absolutely sure they want to take on this great responsibility. Owning a dog, particularly an Australian cattle dog, takes a great commitment and it is not something that should ever be done on a whim. The hasty purchase of a dog can result in sheer drudgery and frustration for the owner, and an unhappy situation for the dog itself.

Failure to understand the amount of time and consideration a well-cared for dog requires is one of the primary reasons for the number of unwanted canines that end their lives in an animal shelter. Given proper consideration beforehand, the purchase of a dog can bring many years of companionship and comfort as well as unconditional love and devotion no other animal can match.

Given proper consideration beforehand, the purchase of an Australian cattle dog can bring many years of companionship and comfort as well as unconditional love and devotion.

Should You Own a Dog?

Consider three very important questions:

1. Does the person who will ultimately be responsible for the dog's day-to-day care really want a dog?

In many active families the woman of the household is the person who will have the ultimate responsibility for the family dog and she may not want any more duties than she already has. Pet care can be an excellent way to teach children responsibility, but beware—in their enthusiasm to have a puppy, children are apt to promise almost anything. It is what will happen after the novelty of owning a new dog has worn off that must be considered.

2. Does the lifestyle and schedule of the household lend itself to the demands of proper dog care?

This means there must always be someone available to see to the dog's basic needs: feeding, exercise, coat care, access to the outdoors when required, and so on.

3. Is the kind of dog being considered suitable for the individual or household?

Very young children can be very rough and unintentionally hurt a young puppy of a small breed. On the other hand, a young dog of a very large or very rambunctious breed like the Australian cattle dog can overwhelm and sometimes injure an infant or small child in an enthusiastic moment. Sharing a tiny apartment with a giant breed can prove extremely difficult for both dog and owner. Toy breeds will have difficulty surviving northern winters if required to live outdoors in unheated quarters. A long-haired dog, while

The conformation of purebred dogs is entirely predictable. The owner of a purebred Australian cattle dog puppy can rest assured that his puppy will grow up to look and act very much like all of its relatives.

17

attractive, is hardly suitable for the individual who spends most outdoor time camping, hunting, or hiking through the woods.

In addition to the above three major questions regarding dog ownership, the prospective dog owner should strongly consider the specific peculiarities of his or her own lifestyle or household. All this applies whether the household is made up of a single individual or a large family. Everyone involved must realize that the new dog will not understand the household routine and must be taught *everything* you want it to know and do. This takes time and patience, and very often the most important lessons for the new dog to learn will take the longest for it to absorb.

Why a Purebred Dog?

There is no difference in the love, devotion, and companionship that a mixed-breed dog and a purebred dog can give its owner. There are, however, some aspects of suitability that can best be fulfilled by the purebred dog.

All puppies, purebred or not, are cute but it stands to reason that not all puppies will grow up to be particularly attractive adults. It is nearly impossible

The Australian cattle dog must be given work to do or it will think up something to do on its own that might not be entirely acceptable.

to predict what a mixed-breed puppy will look like at maturity. Size, length of hair, and temperament can vary widely and may not be at all what the owner had hoped. Then what happens to the dog?

In buying a purebred puppy, the purchaser will have a very good idea of what the dog will look like and how it will behave as an adult; purebred dogs have been bred for generations to meet specifications of conformation and temperament.

When choosing a puppy, one must have the adult dog in mind because the adult dog should fit the owner's lifestyle and esthetic standards. A very fastidious housekeeper may have trouble accommodating a large breed that sheds its coat all year around. Joggers or long-distance runners who want a dog to accompany them are not going be happy with a short-legged or slow breed. It is also important to know that short muzzled dogs and those with "pushed-in" faces have very little heat tolerance. Consider these points *before* you select a puppy.

Since the conformation of purebred dogs is entirely predictable, the owner of a purebred puppy will know that the breed he or she selects will still be appropriate as an adult. Temperament in purebred dogs has great predictability, although there may be minor variations within a breed. The hair-trigger response and hyperactivity of certain breeds would not be at all suitable for someone who wants a quiet, contented companion, nor would the placid attitude of other breeds be desirable for someone who wants an athletic, exuberant dog to frolic with. With purebred dogs, you are reasonably assured of selecting a dog compatible with your lifestyle.

Price

The initial purchase price of a purebred dog will be a significant investment for the owner, but a pure-bred dog costs no more to maintain than a mixed breed. If the cost of having exactly the kind of dog you want and are proud to own is gauged over the number of years you will enjoy it, you will have to admit the initial cost becomes far less consequential.

Appearance

Before hastily buying a breed of dog whose *appearance* you find appealing, spend time with adult members of the breed or do some good research to assure yourself that you and the breed in question are temperamentally compatible. Many books have been written about the various breeds and often devote a good amount of space discussing the temperament of the breed. Visiting kennels or breeders specializing in the breed of your choice will assist you enormously in deciding if you are considering the right breed for you.

Is the Australian Cattle Dog the Right Dog for You?

The Australian cattle dog was bred to work. At no time in its developmental history was any attempt made to make the breed a lapdog or boudoir companion. The cattle dog must be given something to do or it will think up something to do on its own—and that "something" just might be dismantling your new sofa or taking up your wall-to-wall carpeting. The cattle dog needs a lot of exercise. It is not an apartment dog that can be left alone in confined quarters day after day.

Deciding Who Is Boss

This is definitely a breed with a mind of its own. It will size up a situation and, if unaccustomed to looking to its owner for directions, will make decisions on its own and it will *act*. It has a hair-trigger response mechanism. Owners who have been negligent in making their cattle dog understand who makes all the rules will find themselves left out of decision making entirely. Remember the cattle dog's dingo heritage and its resultant need for a strong pack leader. If you do not provide that leadership, your dog will provide leadership for itself.

It takes a lot of dog to boss around a full-grown wild steer and what the cattle dog lacks in size, it easily makes up in aggression and tenacity. They were bred to *bite* the heels of cattle. The fact that there might not be any cattle heels around to bite does not diminish their desire to do so. If this is unharnessed, there could be a distinct problem.

With all that said, if a prospective owner is willing to take on the responsibilities required of a conscientious cattle dog owner, there are few breeds that can provide more devotion and companionship than this one. The Australian cattle dog lives to be with its owner and it can do that since it is a breed that is just about the right size to go anywhere—not too large and not

The Australian cattle dog was bred to bite the heels of cattle. The fact that there might not be cattle heels available to bite does not diminish their desire to do so. Unharnessed, this could prove to be a problem.

An Australian cattle dog will size up a situation and, if unaccustomed to looking to its owner for directions, will make decisions on its own.

It takes a lot of dog to boss around a full-grown steer, but what the Australian cattle dog lacks in size, it easily makes up in aggression and tenacity.

too small, short of coat and long on endurance, tolerant of both heat and cold. Australian cattle dogs love the water and can swim great distances without tiring. They love their home and do not have an urge to roam.

The cattle dog can be trained to do just about anything a dog is capable of doing, particularly if the task includes agility and enthusiasm. It is a true athlete and brave to a fault. There are no lengths too great for a cattle dog to go in the protection of home and family. Children quickly earn the breed's devotion and protection without trying. In fact, families may sometimes find their children being "protected" from people and situations that they do not even want them protected from!

Male or Female?

While some individuals may have their personal preferences as to the sex of their dog, we can honestly say that both the male and the female Australian cattle dog make equally good companions and are equal in

their trainability and affection. The decision will have more to do with the lifestyle and ultimate plans of the owner than differences between the sexes in the breed.

The male cattle dog is much taller and heavier boned than the female and does present one problem that the prospective buyer should consider. While both the male and the female must be trained not to urinate in the home, the male of any breed of dog has a natural instinct to lift his leg and urinate on objects to establish and "mark" his territory. The degree of effort that must be invested in training the male to not do this varies with the individual dog. This habit becomes increasingly more difficult to correct with the number of times a male dog is used for breeding, as the mating act increases his need and desire to mark his territory.

On the other hand, one must realize that the female is not problem free. She will have her semiannual, and sometimes burdensome, heat cycle

The male cattle dog is normally much taller and heavier-boned than the female.

Children quickly earn the Australian cattle dog's devotion and protection.

after she is eight or nine months old. At these times she must be confined in order to avoid soiling her surroundings, and she must also be closely watched to prevent male dogs from gaining access to her or she will become pregnant.

Altering

Both of these sexually associated problems can be eliminated by having the pet Australian cattle dog "altered" (see Spaying and Neutering, pages 45–46). Spaying the female and neutering the male will not change the personality of your pet and will avoid many problems. Neutering the male cattle dog can reduce its aggressive attitude toward other males and will reduce, if not entirely eliminate, its desire to pursue a neighborhood female that shows signs of an impending romantic attitude. Neutering and spaying also precludes the possibility of your pet adding to the extreme pet overpopulation problem that concerns environmentalists worldwide. Spaying

Good breeding is time-consuming and costly. Good breeders protect their investment by providing the best prenatal care for their breeding females and good nutrition for growing puppies.

also reduces the risk of mammary cancer in the female.

It is important to understand though that these are not reversible procedures. If you are considering the possibility of showing your Australian cattle dog, altered animals are not allowed to compete in American Kennel Club or United Kennel Club conformation dog shows. They may, however, compete in herding and obedience trials, agility events and field trials.

Where to Buy Your Australian Cattle Dog

Your Australian cattle dog will live with you for many years. This is a breed that regularly enjoys a long, healthy life, living to be twelve, fourteen, even sixteen years of age. It is extremely important, therefore, that the dog comes from a source where physical and mental soundness are primary considerations in the breeding program, usually the result of careful breeding over a period of many years. Selective breeding is aimed at maintaining the virtues of the breed and eliminating genetic weaknesses. Because this selective breeding is time-consuming and costly, good breeders protect their investment by providing the best prenatal care for their breeding females and nutrition for the growing puppies. There is no substitute for the amount of dedication and care good breeders give their dogs.

The Australian Cattle Dog Club of America and the American Kennel Club (see Useful Addresses, page 93) can provide the prospective buyer with the names and addresses of responsible individuals who have intelligently bred Australian cattle dogs that are available for sale. Many local pet stores will carry a list of good breeders and can refer you directly to them as well.

Breeders—What to Consider

There is a good chance that there are reputable breeders located nearby who will not only be able to provide the Australian cattle dog you are looking for but who will be able to advise you regularly in proper care and feeding. These breeders normally have the parents and other relatives of the dog you are interested in on the premises. The majority of these breeders will be more than happy to show you their dogs and to discuss the advantages and responsibilities involved in owning the breed. Responsible breeders are as concerned about their stock being placed in the right hands as the prospective buyer is in obtaining a sound and healthy dog.

Health: Do not hesitate to ask questions and to ask to see the breeder's mature dogs. While there are relatively few hereditary defects that occur in Australian cattle dogs, experienced breeders know which hereditary problems exist in the breed and will be happy to discuss them with you. Practically all breeds are subject to inherited ailments and Australian cattle dogs are no exception.

Beware of breeders who tell you that their dogs are not susceptible to inherited diseases or potential problems. I do not mean to imply that all Australian cattle dogs are afflicted with genetic problems, but a reliable breeder will give you the information you are entitled to know regarding the individual dog you are considering. The subsection, Inherited Health Problems and Diseases, beginning on page 68, will give you details on some of the genetic ailments that might exist in this breed.

Temperament and health of the parents of your prospective purchase are of paramount importance. It is important that you see the parents, or at the very least, the mother, of your prospective purchase. If you dislike what you observe in either of them, *look elsewhere!*

Environment: Inspect the environment in which the dogs are raised. Cleanliness is as important to producing good stock as are good pedigrees. The time you spend in researching and inspecting the kennel and the adult dogs it houses may well save you a great deal of money and heartache in the years to come.

All this is not to imply your Australian cattle dog puppy must come from a large kennel. On the contrary, many good puppies are produced by small hobby breeders in their homes. These names may well be included in recommendations from both the American Kennel Club and the Australian Cattle Dog Club of America. These individuals offer the same investment of time, study, and knowledge as the larger kennels and they are just as ready to offer the same health guarantees.

A newspaper advertisement may or may not lead you to a reputable hobby breeder. It is up to you to investigate and compare as you would in the case of any major purchase. Good hobby breeders will sell only to approved buyers and spend considerable time in determining this. If the seller is willing to let you make a purchase with no questions asked, you should be highly suspicious.

Selecting an Australian Cattle Dog Puppy

What to Look For

The Australian cattle dog puppy you want to buy should be a happy, playful extrovert. Never select a puppy that appears frail or sickly because you feel sorry for it. Australian cattle dog puppies with positive temperaments are not afraid of strangers. Under normal circumstances you will have the whole litter in your lap if you kneel and call them to you. When the AKC breed standard states that the Australian cattle dog should be "suspicious of strangers," it is referring to the adult dog. The adult cattle dog has developed territorial tendencies and the "suspicious" part of its nature is simply the dog's desire to protect home or owner from intrusion. A puppy will not have developed this part of its character and you definitely should avoid the puppy that cowers in a corner or one that tries to run away from you.

The Australian cattle dog puppy you select should be a happy, playful extrovert.

Ranchers in Australia have been known to pick their cattle dog puppy from a litter by calling to the puppies and walking away. The pup that reaches the caller first is the one that is chosen. If nothing else, this certainly makes a very strong comment on the fearless and friendly attitude of the well-bred Australian cattle dog puppy.

If one puppy in particular appeals to you, pick it up and, if possible, carry it off to an area nearby where the two of you can spend some time alone. As long as a puppy is still in a fairly familiar environment where scents and sounds are not entirely strange, it should remain relaxed and happy in your arms. Avoid the puppy that becomes tense and struggles to escape.

Physical Signs

When you and your prospective puppy are alone, you will have an opportunity to examine the puppy more closely:
• Check the puppy's ears. They should be pink and clean. Any odor or dark discharge could indicate ear mites, which in turn would indicate poor maintenance.
• The inside of the puppy's mouth and gums should be pink, and the teeth should be clean and white. There should be no malformation of the mouth or jaw.
• The dark eyes should be clear and bright. Again, be aware of any signs of discharge.
• Australian cattle dog puppies should feel compact and substantial to the

touch, never bony and undernourished, nor should they be bloated; a taut and bloated abdomen is usually a sign of worms. A rounded puppy belly is normal.

• The nose of an Australian cattle dog puppy should not be crusted or running.

• A cough or diarrhea is a danger signal as are any eruptions on the skin.

• Conformation is important even at an early age. The puppy's legs should be straight. As the pup walks toward you, its front legs should move directly forward, as should the rear legs when the pup is moving away from you. The movement should be free and easy.

If you have been reading and doing your research, you can expect the Australian cattle dog puppy to look almost like a miniaturized version of an adult. The puppy coat is much softer than the adult coat but the hair should never be long or fluffy. Color and markings will be visible but much lighter than when the puppy matures. Cattle dog puppies are born white and color develops as the puppy matures, darkening until it reaches adulthood.

Ears may already be standing but, if not, simply hold the puppy in your two hands and tilt its head downward. The ears will lie back and this will give you a picture of what the puppy will look like when the ears stand on their own. Ears may seem a bit large at this early stage, but more often than not the puppy will grow into them.

Helpful hint: Put the puppy on the floor and when it is busy investigating its surroundings, make a strange noise. The puppy should react and whirl around to see where the noise is coming from. If it does not react, you should definitely investigate the possibility of deafness. Deafness is a serious congenital defect in the breed. Responsible breeders test their breeding stock and the defect is far less a problem today than it was at one time. A responsible

A healthy puppy's eyes will be clear and bright. Discharge of any kind could be a serious problem.

breeder will discuss the problem with you and insure you that the puppy you buy is sound in that respect.

Best Age for Selection

Raising a puppy is a wonderful experience. Granted, at times it can also be one of the most exasperating experiences you have ever attempted. In the end though, having endured each other through all the trials of puppyhood, you and your Australian

Cattle dog puppies are born white and color develops as the puppy matures, darkening until it reaches adulthood.

cattle dog will forge a bond that has no equal.

Should you decide that you do, in fact, wish to raise this little tyke from infancy to adulthood, be aware that most breeders do not and should not release their puppies until they have had their initial inoculations, which is at about eight to ten weeks of age. While they are nursing, puppies receive temporary immunity to diseases through their mother. Once they have been weaned, they lose this immunity and must be appropriately inoculated. Do not remove a puppy from its home environment before it has been vaccinated.

Prior to immunization, puppies are very susceptible to infectious diseases. Many such diseases may be transmitted via the clothing and hands of people. After the first series of vaccinations the breeder will inform you when your Australian cattle dog puppy is ready to leave its first home.

Show Dog or Companion?

If dog shows and breeding are in the future of your Australian cattle dog puppy, the older it is at the time of selection the more likely you will know how good a dog you will have at maturity. The most any breeder can say about an eight-week-old cattle dog puppy is that it has or does not have "show potential." If you are seriously interested in having an Australian cattle dog puppy of the quality to show or to breed, wait with your selection until the puppy is at least five to six months old. By this time, you can be far more certain of dentition, soundness, and attitude, as well as other important characteristics. No matter what you have in mind for your dog's future— dog shows, cattle dog, or nothing more than loving companionship—all of the foregoing should be considered carefully and, above all, temperament of the puppy and of its parents must be a paramount factor in deciding which Australian cattle dog to take home.

If the excitement and pride of owning a winning show dog appeals to you, we strongly urge you to seek out a successful breeder who has a record of having produced winning dogs through the years. As stated, it is extremely difficult, if not impossible, to predict what an eight-week-old puppy will look like as an adult. An experienced breeder, however, will know whether a young puppy has "potential." Unfortunately, most prospective owners want both a very young puppy and some guarantee that the puppy will grow up to be a winning show dog but it is not possible to give that kind of guarantee, and no honest breeder will do so.

Show-prospect Puppies

A show-prospect puppy must not only adhere to all the health and soundness qualifications of the good pet puppy, it must show every sign that it will conform very closely to the rigid demands of the breed standard (see pages 13–15) when it matures. It might make little difference to you if your pet is a bit longer in body or shorter on leg than the ideal set up in the breed standard but faults like this make considerable difference in determining the future of a show dog.

All male show dogs must have two normal-sized testicles in the scrotum. Some males have only one testicle, which eliminates them from being considered as a show prospect. Certainly this would make no difference to pet owners who will have their male dog sexually altered anyway; therefore, purchasing a male with this "fault" could give the buyer a beautiful dog that is not otherwise affordable.

Your chances of obtaining an Australian cattle dog puppy that will mature into a winning adult are far better if purchased from a breeder whose bloodline has produced many champions. Even at that, no one can be sure of having a winner until the puppy has reached maturity. Obviously, a puppy that is six or seven months old, or a young adult will provide much more certainty.

We have known some people who have spent thousands of dollars buying very young puppies again and again but have never achieved their goal of owning a winning show dog. Granted, an older puppy or grown dog may initially cost considerably more than an eight-week-old puppy, but odds are much greater that in the end you will have what you actually wanted.

Experienced and successful Australian cattle dog breeders have spent years developing a line of top-quality animals. These breeders know what to look for in the breed and they are particularly familiar with the manner in which their own stock matures.

Price

The price of an Australian cattle dog puppy can vary considerably but it should be understood that reputable breeders have invested considerable time, skill, and work in making sure they have the best possible breeding stock, all of which costs a great deal of money. Good breeders have also invested substantially in veterinary supervision and testing to keep their stock as free from hereditary defects as possible.

A puppy purchased from an established and successful breeder may cost a few dollars more initially, but the small additional investment can save many trips to the veterinarian over the ensuing years. It is heartbreaking to become attached to a dog only to lose it at an early age because of some health defect.

You should expect to pay $500 or more for an eight-week-old, pet-quality Australian cattle dog puppy. Older puppies will cost more. Youngsters

with show and breeding potential may be double that price and young show stock that has reached the five or six-month-old stage will be even more expensive.

Veterinary Health Check

A responsible breeder will be more than happy to supply a written agreement that the sale of a puppy is contingent upon the puppy's successfully passing a veterinary health check. If the location of the breeders, your home, and your prospective veterinarian allow it, plan the time of day you pick up your puppy so that you can go directly from the breeder to the veterinarian. If this is not possible, you should plan the visit as soon as possible. No longer than 24 hours should elapse before this is done. Should the puppy not pass the veterinary health check, a responsible and ethical breeder will be more than happy either to refund your money or provide you with another puppy depending on the stipulations of the contract.

What You Must Get with Your New Puppy

Inoculations and Health Certificates

By twelve weeks of age most puppies have been vaccinated against hepatitis, leptospirosis, distemper, parainfluenza, and canine parvovirus. Rabies inoculations are usually not given until the puppy is six months of age. There is a set series of inoculations developed to combat these and other infectious diseases and more details are given in the chapter Medical Problems, beginning on page 63.

You are entitled to have a record of these inoculations when you purchase your puppy. Most breeders will give you complete documentation, along with dates on which your puppy was wormed and examined by the veterinarian. Usually, this record will also

A young cattle dog puppy's ears may already be standing up or the puppy may have one up and one down. As the puppy matures both ears will stand erect.

indicate when booster shots are required. These are very important records to keep safe—they will be needed by the veterinarian you choose to care for your Australian cattle dog.

Pedigree and Registration Certificate

Buying a purebred dog also entitles you to a copy of the dog's pedigree and registration certificate. These are two separate documents. The former is simply the dog's family tree and lists

Deafness is a serious congenital defect in Australian cattle dogs. A good test of a puppy's hearing is to make a strange noise when the puppy is busy investigating its surroundings. The puppy should whirl around to see where the noise is coming from.

the registered names of your Australian cattle dog's sire and dam along with their ancestors for several generations.

The registration certificate is issued by the American Kennel Club. When ownership of your cattle dog is transferred from the breeder's name to your name, the transaction is entered on this certificate, and, once mailed to the AKC, it is permanently recorded in their computerized records. The AKC will send you a copy of the duly recorded change. File this document in a safe place along with your other important papers, as you will need it should you ever wish to show or breed your Australian cattle dog.

It is important to understand that the pedigree is simply a listing of the dog's ancestors. The fact that a dog has a pedigree means only that it is purebred, that all of its ancestors are, in fact, Australian cattle dogs. The pedigree does not mean a dog is of superior or show quality. All of the dogs in the pedigree could have been of strictly pet quality. On the other hand, the pedigree could just as well be made up of Australian cattle dogs that have won many show ring titles.

Diet Sheet

A sound and healthy Australian cattle dog puppy is in that condition because it has been properly fed and cared for. Every breeder has a slightly different approach to successful nutrition, so it is wise to obtain a written record or description that details the amount and kind of food your puppy has been receiving. It should also indicate the number of times a day your puppy has been accustomed to being fed and the kind of vitamin supplementation it has been receiving. Maintaining this system at least for the first week or two after your puppy comes home with you will reduce the chances of digestive upsets and loose stools. A good diet program also

The purebred dog's pedigree assures you that all of the individual dogs in its family tree are purebred as well.

projects increases in food and changes that should be made in the dog's diet as it matures.

Consider an Adult Dog

A very young puppy is not your only option for adding an Australian cattle dog to your household. For some people, especially the elderly, a housebroken adult can be an excellent choice. Also, if time available to housebreak is limited, or the owner expects to be away from home frequently, an adult cattle dog can be a wise choice.

Many animal behaviorists place the Australian cattle dog among the most trainable and versatile of all the canine breeds.

Most adult Australian cattle dogs are ready, willing, and capable of learning the household routine.

An important point to consider, however, is that when you buy an Australian cattle dog puppy, the two of you will work into your exercise and training regimen gradually. If you buy an adult, exercise and education start the next morning!

If, in fact, your Australian cattle dog will be a working cattle dog, buying a young adult or even one fully matured that has been trained may be just the answer. A trained cattle dog knows what it has been taught and will perform well for a new owner so long as the new owner has learned how to give commands properly.

Practically all Australian cattle dogs, even adults, seem to adapt to their new environments very easily. This cannot be said for all other breeds. The mature cattle dog also needs far less supervision than a puppy, because it has normally passed through the mischievous stage and the need to chew. Usually, an adult Australian cattle dog is ready, willing, and capable of learning the household routine.

There are some important things to consider in bringing an adult Australian cattle dog into your home:
• The adult dog may have developed habits that you do not find acceptable. In some cases it may be difficult to retrain such animals. Until you begin to work together, there is no way of knowing how willing an adult Australian cattle dog is to learn new habits. Always take an adult dog home on a trial basis to see how it works out for both you and the dog.
• Another factor to consider is that some adult Australian cattle dogs may never have been exposed to or interacted with small children. If there are young children in your home, the first sight of these "miniature people" can be very perplexing to the inexperienced Australian cattle dog, especially loud and very active children. When children run and play, the herding and heeling instinct in the dog may be aroused; perhaps leading to nipping at the children's feet and ankles. It may take considerable time and patience to overcome this inborn instinct but with perseverance and good judgment most cattle dogs can be retrained.

Importance of a Training Regimen

The Australian cattle dog was bred to do a job and in order for it to learn to do its job, it had to inherit a capacity to be trained. Many animal behaviorists place the Australian cattle dog among the most trainable and versatile of all the canine breeds. While certainly a great asset when properly channeled, this capacity left untapped can result in an extremely troublesome, often neurotic dog. The prospective cattle dog owner must be totally committed to establishing and regularly following a training regimen with the dog he or she buys.

Basic obedience training is not a matter of choice in Australian cattle dog ownership—it is a matter of absolute necessity. Anyone who is not willing to invest the time and effort to provide his or her Australian cattle dog with the training it needs should really look to another breed. It makes no more sense to own a dog with a great capacity to work and learn and have it lie idly about than it would to own a high-performance race car that is used only to drive a block or two to the market once a week.

There is no question as to the trainability and intelligence of the Australian cattle dog. The only question that remains is the owner's willingness and ability to provide the proper training and environment.

Care of the Australian Cattle Dog Puppy

Preparing for the New Puppy

There is a great deal you can do prior to your puppy's arrival to make the transition painless and trauma-free. If possible, visit your puppy several times while it is still in its original home so that you are not entirely a stranger.

Well in advance of the puppy's arrival you can secure the equipment and toys that will be needed and prepare the area in which it will initially live. A fenced-off area in the kitchen is the ideal place to start your puppy off; accidents can be easily cleaned up and the kitchen is a room in which there is normally a good deal of traffic. Don't forget, a young puppy is accustomed to the companionship of its littermates, and without them the puppy will be lonely. It will be up to you to compensate for the loss of your puppy's siblings.

Equipment and Toys

The following is a list of the basic requirements you should already have satisfied when your puppy arrives. The value and use of each will be more fully explained as we proceed.

Partitioned-off living area: Paneled fence partitions about four feet (122 cm) high are available at most major pet shops and are well worth the investment for keeping the puppy where you want it to be. Australian cattle dog puppies love to be where their owners are but puppies should not be underfoot.

Cage or shipping kennel: Inside the fenced-off area there should be a wire cage or fiberglass shipping kennel (the open door of which provides access to a sleeping "den"). This cage will also be used for housebreaking (see page 39). These wire cages and fiberglass shipping kennels come in varying sizes. The number 400 size, which is approximately 36 inches long (92 cm) by 24 inches (61 cm) wide by 26 inches (66 cm) high, will be the ideal size to accommodate an Australian cattle dog through adulthood.

Water dish and feeding bowl: These are available in many different materials. Choose something nonbreakable and not easy to tip over—Australian cattle dog puppies very

Choose something nonbreakable and sturdy when selecting water and feeding bowls.

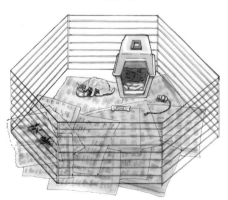

In advance of the puppy's arrival, one should prepare a fenced-off area in the kitchen.

The ideal size kennel for the adult Australian cattle dog can be partitioned off to accommodate the needs of a puppy.

quickly learn to upset the water bowl and relish turning their entire living area into a swimming pool! We recommend stainless steel bowls as they eliminate the worry of toxic content of some plastics and are not as easily chewed and destroyed.

Food recommended on the "diet sheet": In the unlikely circumstance that you were not provided with this information by the puppy's breeder, there are many highly nutritious commercial brands of dog food available at pet stores and supermarkets that come complete with feeding instructions. Veterinarians are always helpful in this area as well.

Brush and comb: A young Australian cattle dog's coat does not require a great deal of grooming, but grooming is important and the process should begin early. Equipment that you will need is described in detail in the chapter Bathing, Grooming, and Home Health Care beginning on page 56.

Soft collar and a leash: There are soft fabric collars that weigh next to nothing that can be purchased at any pet shop. These are ideal for the beginning lessons in that a collar of this type can barely be felt when it is around the puppy's neck. Light weight plastic or fabric leashes are good for the young puppy because they will not weigh heavily on the puppy's neck.

Toys: These can be anything you choose, but be sure they are safe— without buttons or strings that can be chewed off or swallowed. The Australian cattle dog has incredible strength in its jaws, even as a puppy, and can easily demolish things other dogs can not! Also, avoid hard plastic toys that can splinter. Make sure all

The Australian cattle dog puppy has incredible strength in its jaws and can easily demolish things other dogs cannot.

Toys for the Australian cattle dog puppy should never have buttons or strings that can be chewed off or swallowed. Rope toys and Kong chew toys are ideal for the cattle dog puppy.

A young puppy is accustomed to the companionship of its littermates and without them the puppy will be lonely. It will be up to the new owner to compensate for the loss of the puppy's siblings.

When your puppy arrives at its new home it will be confused and lonely, especially at night. Placing the puppy in a box next to your bed allows you to drop a reassuring hand down to the puppy should it wake up crying in loneliness.

toys are larger than those that the puppy can get into its mouth; small toys can become lodged in the mouth and caught in the throat. Do not give your cattle dog puppy old and discarded shoes or socks to play with. A puppy is unable to determine the difference between "old" and "new" and unless carefully watched may think it is perfectly all right to add newly acquired dancing slippers to its toy collection.

Bringing Your Puppy Home

The safest way to transport the puppy from the kennel to your home is to obtain a pet carrier or cardboard box large enough for the puppy to stretch out comfortably with sides that are high enough so that it can not climb out. Put a layer of newspapers at the bottom in case of accidents and a soft blanket or towel on top of that. Ideally, another family member or friend should accompany you to do the driving or hold the carrier that the puppy is in.

Helpful hint: When your puppy arrives at its new home it will be confused and undoubtedly whine in search of its littermates, especially at night when its littermates are not there to snuggle up to. For the first few nights after the new puppy arrives, we put a box next to the bed and let the newcomer sleep there. Should the puppy wake up crying in loneliness, a reassuring hand can be dropped down into the box and we have avoided having to trudge to a different part of the house to quiet the lonely puppy.

Letting the puppy "howl it out" can be a nerve-racking experience that could easily cost you, your family, and your neighbors nights of sleep. Should you wish to transfer the puppy's sleeping quarters to a different part of the house later, you can do this more easily once the puppy has learned to be by itself for increasing periods of time.

HOW-TO:
Basic Puppy Training

Early Training

Simple basic training should begin just as soon as you bring your puppy home. It must be remembered, however, that a young puppy's attention span is very short and puppies are incapable of understanding or retaining complex commands.

It should also be noted here that as rugged a breed as the Australian cattle dog is, it is very sensitive to correction and a stern scolding is usually sufficient to get your point across. Striking an Australian cattle dog (or any other dog) is never necessary; in fact, it is apt to have exactly the opposite effect intended. There are occasions when you may have to take sterner measures but they can normally be taken care of by grabbing your dog by the ruff on both sides of the neck just behind the head and giving the dog a very firm and sharp *"No!"*

Learning the Meaning of *"No!"*

Probably the most important single command your dog will ever learn is the word *"No!"* Never use the word unless you are prepared to enforce it. This is the only way the puppy will understand its meaning, and once understood, it can and will save both you and the puppy a great deal of unnecessary trauma.

The very first time your puppy nips at someone's heels (including your own), you must correct the puppy with a very firm "No!" The Australian cattle dog has a barely suppressible urge to bite at heels and while this may be cute behavior for an eight-week-old puppy, it is downright dangerous for an adult Australian cattle dog to do this. Puppy growling and biting falls under the same heading. Do not let it get started. As with all unwanted behavior in dog training, avoidance is more than half the battle.

The *Come* Command

The next most important lesson for the puppy to learn is to come when called. It is critical, therefore, that the puppy become familiar with its name as soon as possible. Learning to come when called could well save your dog's life when the two of you venture out into the world. *Come,* the command a dog must understand, has to be obeyed always and instantly, but the dog should not associate that command with fear. The dog's responding to its name and the word *Come* should always be associated with a pleasant experience such as great praise and petting or a food treat.

In dog training of any kind it is much easier to avoid the establishment of bad habits than it is to correct entrenched, undesirable behavior. Never give the *Come* command unless you are sure your puppy will come to you. Initially, use the command when the puppy is already on its way to you or give the command while walking away from the youngster.

Very young puppies will normally want to stay as close to their owner as possible, especially in strange surroundings. When your puppy sees you moving away, its natural inclination will be to get close to you. This is a perfect time to use the *Come* command.

Later, as the puppy grows more independent and perhaps

If stern measures are necessary to correct bad habits, hold your Australian cattle dog by the ruff on both sides of the neck just behind the head and give a very firm, "No!"

a bit headstrong, you may want to attach a long leash or rope to the puppy's collar to insure the correct response. Chasing or punishing your puppy for not obeying the *Come* command in the initial training stages makes the youngster associate the command with something negative and will result in avoidance rather than the immediate positive response you desire. It is imperative that you praise your puppy when it does come to you, even if it delays responding for many minutes.

Leash Training

It is never too early to accustom the puppy to a collar and leash; it is your way of keeping your dog under control. It may not be necessary for the puppy or adult dog to wear its collar and identification tags within the confines of your home and property, but no dog should ever leave home without a collar and without the leash held securely in your hand.
• Begin getting your puppy accustomed to its collar by leaving it on for a few minutes at a time. Gradually extend the time you leave the collar on. Most puppies become accustomed to their collar very quickly and forget they are even wearing it.
• Once this is accomplished, attach a lightweight leash to the

It is never too early to accustom the puppy to a collar and leash. Do not try to guide your puppy at first. The point is to accustom the puppy to the feeling of the collar and leash.

collar while you are playing with the puppy in the house or in your yard. Do not try to guide the puppy at first. The point here is to accustom the puppy to the feeling of having something attached to the collar.
• Encourage the puppy to follow you as you move away. Should it be reluctant to cooperate, coax it along with a treat of some kind. Hold the treat in front of the puppy's nose to encourage it to follow you. As soon as the puppy takes a few steps toward you, praise it enthusiastically and continue to do so as you move along.

• Make the initial session very brief and very enjoyable. Continue the lessons in your home or yard until the puppy is completely unconcerned about the fact that it is on a leash. With a treat in one hand and the leash in the other you can begin to use both to guide the puppy in the direction you wish to go.
• Once the collar and leash are accepted you can begin your walks near to the house and eventually around the block. You and your Australian cattle dog puppy are on your way to a lifetime of adventure together.

As rugged a breed as the Australian cattle dog is, it is very sensitive to correction and a stern scolding is usually sufficient to get your point across.

Socialization and Safety

It is very important that you accustom the Australian cattle dog puppy to everyday events as soon as it is practical. Strange noises, children, and other animals can be very frightening when the puppy first encounters them.

Some breeders make it a point to expose their puppies to as many everyday sights and sounds as

Children should be educated about what they may and may not do with the new puppy.

possible, but this is not always practical when there are many dogs to be taken care of. Therefore, it is up to you to gently and gradually introduce your puppy to such sounds as the garbage disposal, the vacuum cleaner, and the television set.

Ideally, the first time your puppy is exposed to a strange, loud sound you will be able to keep the sound limited to just a few seconds. Once the puppy learns that the sound does not present danger, you will be able to increase the length of time. Eventually the puppy will take even the loudest sounds completely in stride.

Young Children

Regardless of whether the cattle dog puppy has had prior experience with young children, the children themselves must be educated about what they may and may not do with the new puppy. Learning the gentle approach and exercising caution when the puppy is underfoot are things all children should know. In the case of an Australian cattle dog puppy, children should not encourage playful "puppy bites" or having the puppy chase them in fun. These are things that may become extremely difficult to correct as the puppy matures.

"Puppy-proofing" Your Home

A good part of your puppy's safety depends upon your ability to properly "puppy-proof" your home. Electrical outlets, lamp cords, strings, and mouth-size objects of any kind all spell danger to the inquisitive puppy. If you think of your new arrival as equal parts building inspector, vacuum cleaner, and demolition expert you will be better equipped to protect your puppy.

Australian cattle dog puppies can be ingenious at getting into places they shouldn't be. Things like household cleaning products, gardening supplies and poisonous plants should be kept in securely latched cupboards or well above a puppy's reach. Most veterinarians will be able to supply you with a list of plants that are poisonous to dogs.

There is a product called Bitter Apple that tastes just like it sounds—*terrible!* Actually a furniture cream, it is nonpoisonous and can be used to coat electrical wires and chair legs. In most (not all) cases, it will deter your puppy from damaging not only household items but itself as well. Should Bitter Apple not work, there is plastic tubing available at hardware stores that can be put around electrical cords and some furniture legs. Still, a bored and restless Australian cattle dog puppy can chew through plastic tubing quicker than most of us are capable of putting it down so never underestimate the ability of your puppy to get into mischief!

There are baby gates to keep your puppy out and cages and kennels of various kinds to keep your puppy in. All this and a daily "Puppy-proofing Patrol" will help you and your pet avoid serious damage and potential danger.

Lifting and Carrying Your Puppy

Learning to pick up and carry the very young cattle dog puppy properly is very important for both adult and child. You should pick up the puppy with one hand supporting its rear and hindquarters and the other hand under the puppy's chest. This gives the puppy a feeling of security and enables you to keep full control. A puppy should *never* be picked up by its front legs or by the scruff of the neck.

Only children old enough to safely hold and control a puppy should be allowed to pick it up. Australian cattle dog puppies are very strong for their size and can suddenly squirm and attempt to jump down out of a child's arms. A fall from any height can seriously and permanently injure a puppy.

Children should never encourage playful "puppy bites" or allow the puppy to chase them in fun. These behaviors are extremely difficult to correct as the puppy grows up.

It is important that everyone in the family learns how to pick up and carry the puppy properly.

The New Puppy and Other Pets

The Australian cattle dog puppy's introduction to older and/or larger dogs in the household must also be carefully supervised. The average cattle dog puppy loves the world and all creatures in it; however, even at a very early age it is inclined to be a little bossy. The adult dog "with seniority" may consider the new youngster an intrusion and mistake its exuberance for aggression. For this reason it is very important to confine the newcomer so that the older dog is not constantly harassed before it has had time to fully accept the puppy. The partitioned area set up to accommodate the new puppy that we described earlier will give the senior member of the canine contingent an opportunity to inspect the new arrival at his or her leisure without having to endure unsolicited attention.

Given their "druther's" an Australian cattle dog prefers to be the only canine on its premises. On the other hand, many cattle dog owners tell of their dogs getting along famously with resident dogs, cats, even other small animals—even to the point of appointing themselves guardians and protectors.

Car Travel

A part of an Australian cattle dog puppy's socialization process will take place away from home. The puppy must learn to accept strange people and places, and the only way for the puppy to learn to take these changes in stride is to visit as many new sites and meet as many strangers as you can arrange. Trips to the shopping mall or walks through the park will expose your young cattle dog to new and different situations each time you are out. Of course this should never be attempted until your puppy has had all of its inoculations. Once that is completed, you are both ready to set off to meet the world and this often involves riding in a car.

Most adult Australian cattle dogs love to ride in a car. The moment they hear those car keys jingle they are ready and willing to go. Some puppies, however, unfortunately suffer varying degrees of motion sickness. The best way to overcome this problem, should it exist, is to begin with very short rides, such as once around the block. Ending the ride with a fun romp, or a little food treat helps make the ride something to be enjoyed. The puppy should not be fed a full meal before the ride.

When the puppy seems to accept these short rides happily, the length of time in the car can be increased gradually until you see that the puppy is truly enjoying the outings. Even those dogs and puppies suffering the most severe cases of carsickness seem to respond to this approach and soon begin to consider the car a second home.

Words of Caution on Dogs and Cars

As much as it might seem more enjoyable to have your Australian cattle dog puppy or adult ride loose in the car, this can be extremely dangerous. An overly enthusiastic canine passenger can interfere with the driver's control or divert the driver's attention. Also, a sudden stop can hurl your dog against the front window, severely injuring or even killing it.

The safest way to transport your cattle dog is in a carrier with the door securely latched. There are also cars such as station wagons that accommodate partitions commonly referred to as "dog guards." These safety devices confine dogs to the rear portion of the car. Employing these simple safety precautions might one day save the life of your pet.

Tags: Another important travel tip is to make sure your canine companion is wearing a collar with identification tags attached. In fact, whenever your cattle dog is not at home with you, it should be wearing a collar with identification tags. Many times, a dog is thrown clear of the car in an accident but becomes so frightened that it runs blindly away. Not knowing where it is and not carrying any means of identification, the dog may be lost forever.

Closed windows: It is probably best to avoid leaving your dog alone in a car at anytime. However, if you must leave your dog alone, make it a practice to keep the windows at least partially open. Even on cool days the sun beating down on a closed car can send the inside temperature soaring. Leaving an Australian cattle dog alone in an unventilated car could easily cause its death.

A cattle dog should never leave home without a collar and identification tag.

Housebreaking

Previously we mentioned the great value in getting your Australian cattle dog accustomed to a wire cage or fiberglass shipping kennel. These containers are commonly called crates by dog breeders and are invaluable in housebreaking your dog.

It has been our experience that new dog owners will initially look upon the crate method of confinement during housebreaking as cruel, but more often than not, these same people come back to thank us for suggesting the crate method as one of the most valuable training tips they have ever learned. Using a crate reduces the average housebreaking time to a minimum and eliminates keeping the puppy under constant stress by correcting it for making mistakes in the home. Most dogs, and Australian cattle dogs in particular, continue to use their crates voluntarily as a place to sleep, as it provides a sense of safety and security. It becomes their cave or den and in many cases a place to store their favorite toys or bones.

Those of us who live in an earthquake-prone area find our dogs will make a hasty retreat to their crate at the earliest sign of a tremor. Often we have found it necessary to become very persistent in order to get some dogs to emerge from their crate even after the quake has long passed.

Confining your dog is the only possible way to avoid having soiling accidents in the house. Australian cattle dogs are instinctively clean animals and will not soil their immediate surroundings unless they have no choice.

The Crate Method

The crate used for housebreaking should not be too large or the puppy will sleep at one end and eliminate in the other. It should be large enough for the puppy to stretch out comfortably as well as stand up and turn around easily. Naturally, this creates a problem, as the proper size crate for an eight-week-old puppy will not be the proper size for a six-month-old puppy. The easiest way to solve this is to use a piece of plywood to block off a part of the crate, adjusting the space accordingly as the puppy grows.

The average cattle dog puppy loves the world and all creatures in it; however, even at a very early age it is inclined to be a little bossy around other, even older, animals.

Feeding in the Crate

Begin using the crate by feeding the puppy in it. Close and latch the door while the puppy is eating. As soon as the food has been consumed, unlatch the crate door and *carry* the puppy outdoors to the place where you want it to eliminate. Should you not have access to the outdoors, or feel you will later not be able to provide outdoor access for the housebroken dog, place newspapers or some other absorbent material in an out-of-the-way place that will remain easily accessible to the dog. Do *not* let the puppy run around or play after eating until you have carried it to the designated area. It is extremely difficult to teach a puppy not to eliminate indoors once it has begun to do so; therefore, it is very important to prevent accidents rather than correct them.

Being Consistent

Young puppies will void both bowel and bladder almost immediately after eating, after strenuous play, and upon waking from a night's sleep or even a nap. Being aware of this will save a good many accidents. If, after each of these activities, you consistently take the puppy to the place designated for eliminating, you will reinforce the habit of going there for that purpose.

Only after seeing that the puppy has relieved itself in both ways should you allow the puppy to play unconfined and then only while you are there to watch what is happening. Should the puppy begin to sniff the floor and circle around or squat down to relieve itself, say *"No!,"* pick it up immediately, and take it to the designated place.

When you are not able to watch what the puppy is doing indoors, it should be in the crate with the door latched. Each time you take the puppy to its crate, throw a small food treat into the crate and praise the puppy as it enters the crate to go after the treat. If the puppy starts whining, barking, or scratching at the door because it wants to be let out, it is crucial that you do not submit to those demands. The puppy must learn not only to stay in its crate, but also to do so without complaining unnecessarily.

Every time the puppy begins to whine or bark say *"No!"* very firmly. If necessary, give the crate a sharp rap with a rolled-up newspaper. It may take a good bit of persistence on your part, but patience will win out in the end.

Developing a Schedule

It is important to realize that a puppy of eight to twelve weeks will have to relieve its bladder every few hours except at night; therefore, you

When to Take Your Puppy Outdoors
- Very first thing in the morning.
- Immediately after eating.
- Immediately after drinking.
- Right after a nap.
- When it circles and sniffs the floor.
- Right after playtime.
- When it gets that "perplexed," anxious look.
- When it starts to squat.

must adjust your schedule and the puppy's accordingly. You must also be sure your puppy has entirely relieved itself at night just before you retire and be prepared to attend to this the very first thing in the morning when you awake. How early in the morning your puppy needs its first outing will undoubtedly be determined by the puppy itself, but do not expect the young puppy to wait very long for you to respond to its "I have to go out now" signals. You will quickly learn to identify the difference between a puppy's signals that nature is calling and those that indicate it simply does not want to be confined.

Care and persistence in this project pays off very quickly with practically all Australian cattle dog puppies, and eventually you will begin to detect a somewhat anxious look or attitude in the puppy that indicates that it needs to relieve itself. Even the slightest indication in this direction should be met with immediate action on your part and accompanied with high praise and positive reinforcement.

When the Owner Is Away

The crate method of housebreaking is without a doubt the simplest and quickest method I have ever found to housebreak a puppy. It is obvious, however, that this method cannot be used if you must be away from home all day or for even many hours at a time. Everyone has an occasional day away from home but if these prolonged absences are to occur daily, the cattle dog puppy is not the ideal "home alone" candidate. We repeat—the Australian cattle dog was bred to work and to be with its owner. Neither of its basic needs can be fulfilled living in a home where the dog's owner is absent day in and day out. Serious emotional problems can result.

Again, we must stress that young puppies cannot contain themselves for long periods of time. If the puppy must regularly be left alone for more than two or three hours at most, an alternative method must be used, but confinement is still the operative word for success.

For obvious safety reasons, an Australian cattle dog puppy should never be left to roam the house while the owners are away. It is dangerous for the puppy and accidents are bound to happen. The fenced-off area in the kitchen recommended for the arrival of the new puppy is the ideal place of confinement for your puppy while you are gone. The space should be only large enough to permit the puppy to eliminate away from the place in which it sleeps. The entire kitchen area is normally too large a space and creates the eliminating at random habit that is to be avoided at all cost.

The floor of the fenced-off area should be lined with newspaper. The puppy will become accustomed to relieving itself on the newspaper and this should become the "designated spot" to which you will take your puppy when you are home and the puppy indicates it has need to eliminate. When you are home, you must insist the puppy use the newspapers every time.

Care of the Adult Australian Cattle Dog

Prepare for an Active Dog

There are some breeds that do well living outdoors in a run or in a kennel with only minimal human contact. There are others that are perfectly content to lounge on the sofa all day while their owners are away from morning to night. Rest assured, the Australian cattle dog is neither! Its entire genetic makeup urges it to be continually active both mentally and physically. If you as an owner accommodate this activity, you will have a dog that will at times amaze you with its intelligence and readiness to learn. If you do not work with your Australian cattle dog there is little doubt that behavioral problems will develop.

Most owners are quick to agree that failure to provide an Australian cattle dog with something to do will definitely inspire it to become quite creative on its own. That creativity, unfortunately, might prove terribly costly to the negligent owner and the cattle dog's determined nature will not have that behavior easily dissuaded.

Helpful hint: Plan on giving your Australian cattle dog time to "work." That work can take the form of allowing your dog to perform its obedience repertoire, playing flyball or frisbee, or perfecting its agility or herding exercises. These activities are described in greater detail in the chapter titled, Sharing Your Life with an Australian Cattle Dog, beginning on page 69. This, combined with daily walks, grooming sessions, and simply having your Australian cattle dog sit beside you while you watch television or read will satisfy your dog's need for activity and human contact.

Outdoor Manners

Since a good part of the time you spend with your cattle dog will be outdoors, consideration must be given to keeping your dog under control at all times. As previously stated, always use a leash and collar and make sure the identification tags are securely attached to the collar.

Use of a leash is particularly important when your cattle dog will be near children. Young children are high-energy individuals and there is no way nor any need to keep them from running and being noisy. This will awaken every herding instinct an uncontrolled cattle dog possesses and the unrestrained dog could well run off herding the children and biting at their heels.

An Australian cattle dog may not be inherently quarrelsome but it will not take aggression on the part of another dog lightly. You must have your dog under control at all times, even though other people may not be equally responsible.

Never let your dog relieve itself where people might walk or children are playing. Try to teach it to use the gutter to relieve itself. Even then, you should always carry a small plastic bag to remove droppings immediately and dispose of them in a trash receptacle. Many city governments impose heavy fines on dog owners who do not pick up after their dogs.

Dealing with Behavior Problems

Most of the behavior problems owners experience with their Australian cattle dogs are due to the fault of the owner rather than the dog. One must not forget that an Australian cattle dog is first and foremost a dog, and one of the basic needs of all dogs is to have a "pack leader." A pack leader sets boundaries and in so doing gives the members of the pack a sense of security.

Boundary setting and enforcing those boundaries do not intimidate your dog or diminish its capacity to learn. Setting limits actually establishes a line of communication between you and your dog that works for both of you.

Protective and Aggressive Tendencies

An Australian cattle dog will protect its owner and its owner's property at the cost of its own life if need be. This is an admirable quality but here again, unchecked, this tendency can lead to an Australian cattle dog deciding on its own what and how it will protect. Obedience training and an unquestioned willingness to respond to the *No* command are an absolutely necessary part of your dog's education. An Australian cattle dog must understand when and from whom it should protect you; it must understand that *protection does not include aggression!*

Chewing

Puppies will chew. It helps them through their teething stages, and it exercises and strengthens their jaws. Dogs chew things because they enjoy it. Chewing relieves stress and boredom. Your dog must learn early on what it can and cannot chew. Half the battle is in preventing dogs from chewing the wrong things. Don't give your dog the opportunity to do so.

A dog cannot tell the difference between your discarded old slipper and your newest pair of dress shoes; both smell exactly like you and are just as chewable. Don't expect your dog to understand that it is acceptable to chew on one and not the other. Never give your dog any of your personal items to chew on; you must assist the dog's learning that none of the smell-just-like-you items is a plaything.

Make sure your Australian cattle dog is confined to its crate or dog-proof room with something it is allowed to chew when you are not there to supervise. Sound cruel? Think again. Which is more cruel—safely confining your dog when you are not there or flying into a rage because the dog entertained itself by eating a hole in the sofa while you were gone?

Housebreaking Problems

Housebreaking is based upon a dog's natural dislike for eliminating where it eats and sleeps. An Australian cattle dog is a particularly clean dog but supervision is important in having the dog understand human cleanliness rules. A dog does not have to eliminate near its food or sleeping place when given freedom of the whole house. For more on housebreaking, see page 39.

Jumping Up

Even people who like dogs do not particularly enjoy being jumped up on when they enter someone's home. Consistency is the only thing that works here. Do not let your dog jump up on your leg or on anyone else's—ever. A leg is a leg, and if it is acceptable to jump up on yours for a pat, then in the dog's mind all other legs are fair game as well.

When your Australian cattle dog runs joyfully to greet you and jumps up for a pat, give the command *"Off!"* and push its paws off your leg. As soon as the dog's paws hit the floor, praise it lavishly. Everyone in the

Everything in the Australian cattle dog's genetic makeup urges it to be continually active both mentally and physically. If the owner accommodates this activity he or she will have a dog that will amaze with its intelligence and readiness to learn.

family must do this or it will not work. When you and your dog are away from home, have your dog under control on its leash and repeat the command when your dog attempts to jump up on strangers.

Puppies will chew. It helps them through their teething stages and it exercises and strengthens their jaws.

Refusing to Stay "Home Alone"

The Australian cattle dog is a social creature and some of them become more upset at being left alone than others. Some dogs may bark, whine, or attempt to destroy things. All dogs must learn that your absence is simply a matter of routine. Don't treat your departure or return like the climax in a romance novel. Dogs get caught up in your emotional responses. If the dog relates your coming and going with hugging, kissing, and all kinds of heightened emotion, anxiety sets in.

Feeling secure in the kennel or cage you have provided is the first step in your Australian cattle dog's "home alone" training. This nips in the bud any chance of destructive behavior. Going in and out of the room while the dog is confined is the next stage. The dog is learning that you do come back.

Stepping outside the house but remaining within earshot comes next. The minute the barking or howling begins, you must command *No!* Increase the time you are out of sight but not out of earshot. Eventually, your absence will go by unnoticed. This may take longer to accomplish with some dogs than it does with others, but persistence is the key. When being left alone is no longer a traumatic experience, you can experiment with leaving the dog loose in a room or in the house if you wish, but again, this should be done gradually.

Digging

All dogs like to dig. Australian cattle dogs love it! They do it to relieve boredom and to find a nice cool spot to lie in. They do it to seek and destroy vermin they know (or think they know) are hidden under the ground. Correcting the digging problem is not easy.

Again, supervision works best. If it is not possible to supervise your dog while it is outdoors, keep it inside until you can be there to watch what is going on. The minute your dog attempts to dig, let it know with that tried-an- true *No* command that this is not acceptable. Good luck on this one!

Some cattle dog owners have dealt with the digging problem by providing their dogs with a place to do just that. A pit at the back of one's property or in the corner of the yard can be allocated for its digging needs, and with patience and supervision dogs can be trained to understand that their "pit" is the only place digging is allowed. You can encourage your dog to dig in its own pit by burying some delectable "treasures" there. Once or twice, assist the dog in finding what is buried there and give lavish praise when the objects are "found."

Spaying and Neutering

All companion Australian cattle dogs, whether male or female, should be sexually altered unless specifically purchased to breed or to show. Only an Australian cattle dog purchased from a breeder who has recommended that it be bred should be allowed to have offspring. You would be astounded by how many dogs and cats, numbering in the millions, are put to sleep each year because they have no homes.

We trust that you, as a responsible dog owner, would never allow your Australian cattle dog to roam the streets, nor would you consider turning it over to the dog pound. Yet there is no way you can guarantee that someone who might purchase a puppy from you will not be irresponsible and permit the dog to roam or wind up being euthanized at the pound.

Parents who wish to have their young children "experience the miracle of birth" can do so by renting videos of animals giving birth. Handling the experience this way saves adding to pet overpopulation.

Even people who like dogs do not appreciate being jumped on. A cattle dog must be taught that this is not allowed and consistency is the only manner in which the dog will learn this lesson.

There is constant lobbying throughout America to restrict the rights of all dog owners and dog breeders because of this pet overpopulation and the unending need to destroy unwanted animals. Thoughtful dog owners will leave the breeding process to experienced individuals who have the facilities to keep all resulting offspring on their premises until suitable and responsible homes can be found for them.

Altering your pet can also avoid some of the more distasteful aspects of dog ownership. As previously discussed, males that have not been altered have the natural instinct to lift their legs and urinate on objects to mark the territory in which they live. It can be extremely difficult to teach an unaltered male not to do this in your home. Males also have a greater tendency to roam if there is a female in heat in the area.

The female will have two estrus cycles that are accompanied by a bloody discharge. Unless the female is kept confined, there will be extensive soiling of the area in which she is allowed and, much more disastrous, she could become mismated and pregnant. Unspayed females also have a much higher risk of developing pyometra or mammary cancer later in life.

Toys

The rules governing the selection of toys for an Australian cattle dog puppy apply throughout the lifetime of your dog. Never give an Australian cattle dog a toy that is small enough to fit in the dog's mouth or that can be chewed apart into small pieces. Extra consideration must be given to the cattle dog's phenomenal jaw power. A toy that might last some other breed a lifetime can be shattered in minutes by the Australian cattle dog. Very strong rubber rings and toys designed for large dogs are usually suitable for the Australian cattle dog.

Some cattle dogs treasure teddy bears and other stuffed animals and keep them nearly intact for many years; however, in most cases toys of this kind can be dangerous. More than one dog has expressed its displeasure at being left behind by completely dismantling a favorite teddy bear or stuffed doll. The danger here is that the material with which the toy has been stuffed can be ingested and cause severe illness or even death.

Bones

Bones of any kind are not a wise choice for an Australian cattle dog. They can even splinter large knucklebones. Further, if there are any traces of meat on the bone, there is a breeding ground for bacteria and if the bone remains outside, it can attract vermin.

Instilling Good Behavior

Responsible owners will have begun training when their cattle dog arrived (see pages 34–35). Trying to undo bad habits is extremely difficult with any dog and particularly so with this headstrong breed. For instance, a dog that has been permitted to sleep on its owner's bed or climb up on furniture for many months can simply not understand why, starting today, this is no longer allowed.

You may well have a good reason for making this change, but you will be hard-pressed to make your Australian cattle dog understand this reason. What will result instead is a constant war; your cattle dog will do everything in its power to resume its comfortable habit, and you will lose patience with its attempts to do so. If your dog's first attempts to break any household rule are met by your firmly grasping it by the ruff of the neck and a sharp *No!* it is highly unlikely the issue will become a contest of wills.

You need not worry about hurting the dog's feelings so long as you are not unfair, inconsistent, or violent. Aggression on the part of your Australian cattle dog should not be tolerated; avoid allowing it ever to start. Do not permit your puppy ever to growl or snap should you want to take away a toy or pick up its food dish. If you allow this behavior when your dog is a youngster, you can rest assured you will wind up with an Australian cattle dog that will challenge you at every turn as an adult. A sharp rap with your fingers on the nose of the puppy that is testing its dominance by growling or biting will not have any ill affects upon its development. It will, however, go a long way in preventing a dangerous problem from ever getting under way.

An Australian cattle dog cannot be bullied. It will simply not respond to that kind of treatment. Clear consistent rules are what the breed needs and thrives on.

Training Classes

For obedience work beyond the basics described, it can be extremely beneficial for the Australian cattle dog owner to seek out local professional assistance. This can be obtained in many ways. There are free-of-charge classes at Department of Parks and Recreation facilities, as well as very formal and sometimes very expensive individual lessons with private trainers. There are some obedience schools that will take your dog and train it for you; however, we find in the case of Australian cattle dogs that there is no substitute for the rapport that develops when dog and owner train together.

Training classes are especially good for Australian cattle dogs because they give them an opportunity to learn to respond in the midst of strange dogs and strange people. The classes are also a wonderful socialization opportunity for the dogs.

Traveling with Your Dog

At first thought, having your cattle dog accompany you on an extended trip may sound like great fun for both of you, but further consideration could well alter your decision:
• You must ask yourself where your Australian cattle dog will stay when you stop along the way to eat or to sleep. Unlike most European countries, restaurants in America do not permit dogs to accompany their owners inside the establishment.
• Leaving your dog in a parked automobile while you eat can be very dangerous, as weather conditions can change rapidly and temperatures in a closed car can soar.
• Leaving the windows open puts your pet in danger of escaping or being stolen, even if it is safely secured in a traveling container. A slightly open window is of little help once the sun begins to beat down on the car.

Training classes are especially good for the Australian cattle dog because they provide an opportunity for the dog to understand that commands must be obeyed even with strange dogs and strange people present.

• Many hotels and motels do not allow dogs into the rooms because other guests have abused this privilege in the past. Many of the hotels and motels that do allow pets into the rooms charge an extra fee or security deposit. These establishments also assume that your dog is accustomed to being left alone in a strange place and will not disturb other guests by barking and howling while you are out of your room.
• Changing your dog's accustomed food and water can create a number of problems, including diarrhea, not something most people wish to cope with while traveling.

Have a Good Trip

It should be easy to see that taking your Australian cattle dog along with you on a trip will require a great deal of advance planning. An air-conditioned car can help considerably if

47

your trip will be made through areas where daytime temperatures are high. Take the crate or cage with you that you have been using at home. This keeps your pet safe while traveling and provides a safe, secure, and familiar place for the dog if you are out of your hotel room.

Stops along the way must be carefully planned. Realize that your selection of restaurants will have to be made with your pet's safety in mind. At any stop your car must not be left in the sun. Further, unless the weather is very cool, windows should be left open if your dog is in a cage or crate and your car must be where you or a member of your party can see it at all times.

Many people who travel with their pets make an early morning stop at a grocery store or carry-out restaurant and purchase their own food for the day. Meal stops can then be made at some shady spot along the way. Should you decide to do this, it will also give you an opportunity to exercise your dog at the same time.

Dinnertime should come after you have checked into your hotel or motel and put your dog in your room. Reservations must be made in advance with those places that allow dogs in the rooms. If you have taken our previous advice and trained your Australian cattle dog to stay alone in its kennel or cage, you will not have to worry about barking and howling while you are gone, nor will you run the risk of having your dog cause any damage to the room.

Leaving your dog alone: If you have not accustomed your dog to being left alone in its kennel, it is to be hoped that it has at least learned to be left alone. If so, we seriously advise closing your Australian cattle dog in the bathroom while you are out of the room. It is very important to leave a "Do not disturb" sign on your door while you are gone to avoid a

staff person's entering your room. An Australian cattle dog considers guarding your temporary accommodations from intrusion just as important as guarding your regular home.

If your dog will not stay alone in a strange room without barking, *do not leave it alone!* The dog can become frenzied and destroy things or disturb the other occupants of the hotel. You must be considerate of others—both people who are not particularly dog-tolerant as well as those who might wish to stay at the same hotel later with their own dog. The management of the hotel will not be disposed to allow other people with dogs to stay if you have abused your privileges.

Food and water: You must take along an adequate supply of your Australian cattle dog's accustomed food and water. Changing diets and water can seriously upset your dog, and diarrhea and vomiting are the last things you will want to deal with in your hotel room.

Brush and comb: Do take your dog's brush and comb along. If you plan to hike or walk your dog along the side of the road, these accessories will enable you to get rid of any unwanted weeds, seeds, or dirt your Australian cattle dog's coat might have attracted.

Alternatives to Traveling with Touser

Many dog owners are surprised to find their dogs actually *enjoy* their stay in a boarding kennel. An Australian cattle dog would undoubtedly enjoy a week or two in a boarding kennel that allows it to run and play all day in an outdoor fenced enclosure far more than being confined to a hotel room or car.

There are many excellent boarding kennels located around most towns and cities that offer facilities that will satisfy the needs of both you and your dog.

Speak to your veterinarian, friends or clients who are familiar with the boarding operation before leaving your dog.

Should you be convinced that your dog could never be happy in a boarding kennel, there are responsible, bonded and experienced "pet sitters" who will come to your home and stay with your pet while you are away. Your veterinarian may be able to supply you with the names of individuals who are experienced at providing this kind of service. It is always wise to ask for references from the individuals who provide this service and important that the references be checked out thoroughly.

Your Aging Dog

The Australian cattle dog ages remarkably well, and though lifespan does vary from dog to dog, it is not unusual to find many members of this breed alive and active even at 12 and 14 years of age. Some old-timers have maintained their sight and hearing and all their teeth until their final days!

Exercise

There are certain precautions that must be taken with the older Australian cattle dog to keep it happy and healthy. Exercise must be adjusted as your dog gets older and you must take pains to see that it is not pushed beyond its capacity when hiking or playing. This is especially so if there are any signs of arthritis and if exercise makes your old friend limp.

Diet

Your Australian cattle dog's diet must also be adjusted accordingly so that there is less strain on the digestive system. The fat content of the food must be reduced. Today, most major dog food manufacturers take canine aging into consideration and offer diets specifically geared to the senior citizen.

It is not unusual to find many Australian cattle dogs alive and active even at 12 and 14 years of age. Many oldtimers retain their sight and hearing and all of their teeth until their final days.

Your veterinarian can advise you about which diets to choose.

If your Australian cattle dog has been accustomed to one major meal each day it is probably wise to adjust this to two or three smaller meals. It is also absolutely necessary to avoid overweight in the aging dog. The strain of additional weight will certainly shorten its lifespan.

Health Problems

Aging frequently affects the Australian cattle dog's ability to see and hear. If you find your previously obedient cattle dog is failing to respond quickly or not at all to your call, do make concessions for age, but be sure to have your dog checked out by the veterinarian for seeing or hearing problems.

Also, the old Australian cattle dog's patience may wear thin much more quickly than it did when it was a youngster. Puppies and children can prove extremely tiresome to the elderly cattle dog and it is up to the owner not to allow the oldtimer to be subjected to youthful harassment.

Excessive drinking of water can be a sign that the kidneys are not working properly. In some cases this can be a sign that bitches that have not been spayed are developing pyometra, which is an inflammation of the womb, a condition that requires prompt professional treatment.

Veterinary science has developed many new methods that assist your dog to stay healthy even through its final years. Regular checkups will prevent rapid progress of the ailments that could lead to the deterioration of your pet.

The Last Good-bye

There will come a time when your canine friend of many years is no longer able to enjoy life and you must make a very painful decision. Fortunately, when science is no longer able to prevent our pets' suffering or incontinence, we are able to mercifully bring their lives to a close.

Your veterinarian will tell you when the time has come to do this and is able to perform this final act with tenderness and skill. Done professionally, there is no stress to your dog, especially if you are there to hold the dog while the veterinarian administers the injection.

This is never an easy decision to make but carefully considered, it is the kindest action you can take for your canine companion that has given you so many years of love and enjoyment.

Feeding

Your Australian cattle dog can be put on an adult feeding schedule at about ten months of age. This means it will receive one main meal a day, preferably at the same time each evening. This meal is supplemented by a morning snack and for this we highly recommend hard dog biscuits made for large dogs (remember those powerful jaws!). These not only prove to be a much anticipated treat, but do wonders toward maintaining healthy gums and teeth.

There is no simple way to answer the question of what is the best food to give your Australian cattle dog. We have spoken to successful cattle dog breeders in many parts of the world and each breeder seems to have their own tried-and-true method. Probably the best answer to the question is, "feed what works best for the dog." Who can tell you just what food that is? We sincerely recommend you consult with the breeder from whom you purchased your Australian cattle dog and your veterinarian.

Amount to Feed

The correct amount of food to maintain an Australian cattle dog's optimum condition varies as much from dog to dog as it does from human to human. It is impossible to state any specific *amount* of food your dog should be given. Much depends upon how much your dog exercises. An Australian cattle dog that spends the entire day working cattle will need considerably more food than the house dog whose exercise is limited to 20 or 30 minutes a day retrieving a ball.

Generally speaking, the amount of food for a normally active cattle dog is the amount it will eat readily within about fifteen minutes of being given the meal. What your dog does not eat in that amount of time should be taken up and discarded. Leaving food out for extended periods of time can lead to erratic and finicky eating habits.

It must be remembered that the Australian cattle dog was originally bred to be a working cattle dog. Meals were sporadic, of questionable nutritious value, and came only after a long grueling day's work. Today's dog has every bit as big an appetite as its ancestors but usually has far less work to do. The breed can gain weight very easily if not watched and not given a considerable amount of exercise.

A good rule of thumb to follow in determining whether or not an Australian cattle dog is receiving the proper amount of food is closely monitoring the dog's condition. You should be able to feel the ribs and backbone through a slight layer of muscle and fat.

Essential Nutrients

Fresh water and a properly prepared balanced diet containing the essential nutrients in correct proportions is all a healthy dog needs to be offered. If your Australian cattle dog will not eat the food offered, it is because it is either not hungry or ill. If the former is the case, the dog will eat when it is hungry. If you suspect the latter, an appointment with your veterinarian is in order.

Hard dog biscuits made for large dogs are a highly anticipated treat for the cattle dog and are excellent for maintaining healthy gums and teeth.

Dogs, whether Australian cattle dogs or Chihuahuas, are carnivorous (meat-eating) animals, and while the vegetable content of your dog's diet should not be overlooked, a dog's physiology and anatomy are based upon carnivorous food acquisition. Protein and fat are absolutely essential in a dog's diet. The animal protein and fat your dog needs can be replaced by some vegetable proteins, but the amounts and the kind require a better understanding of nutrition than most people have.

There are so many excellent commercial dog foods available today that it seems a waste of time, effort, and money to try to duplicate the nutritional content of these carefully thought-out products by cooking food from scratch. It is important though that you read labels carefully or consult with your veterinarian, who will assist you in selecting the best moist or dry food for your Australian cattle dog.

An Australian cattle dog should never be fed scraps from the table.

It is now possible to buy either canned or dry dog food for dogs living almost any lifestyle, but like all things in life, "you get what you pay for."

Canned Food or Dry?

A great deal of research is conducted by manufacturers of the leading brands of dog food to determine the exact ratio of vitamins and minerals necessary to maintain your dog's well-being. Research teams have determined the ideal balance of minerals, protein, carbohydrates, and trace elements for a dog's well being. Dog food manufacturing has become so sophisticated it is now possible to buy food for dogs living almost any lifestyle from sedentary to highly active. This applies to both canned and dry foods, but like most other things in life, "you get what you pay for." It costs the manufacturer more to produce a nutritionally balanced, high-quality food that is easily digested by a dog than it does to produce a brand that provides only marginal nourishment.

By law, all dog food must list all the ingredients in descending order by weight. The major ingredient is listed first, the next most prominent follows, and so on down the line.

A diet based on meat or poultry (appearing first in the ingredients list) is going to provide more nutrition per pound of food than one that lists a filler grain product as the major ingredient. The diet based on meat and poultry will also cost more than a food heavy in inexpensive fillers.

Whether canned or dry, look for a food in which the main ingredient is derived from meat, poultry, or fish. Remember, you cannot purchase a top-quality dog food for the same price as one that lacks the nutritional value you are looking for. In many cases you will find your Australian cattle dog not only needs less of the better food, but there will be less fecal waste as well.

The Appearance of Dog Food

The better foods are not normally manufactured to resemble products that appeal to humans. A dog does not care that a food looks like a sirloin steak or a wedge of cheese—all a dog cares about is how food smells and tastes. The "looks like" dog foods are manufactured to tempt the dog's owner, but since it is highly unlikely that you will be eating your dog's food, do not waste your money.

Be aware of canned or moist products that have the look of "rich red beef," or dry food that is red in color. In most cases, the color is put there to appeal to you and is achieved through the use of red dye. Dyes and chemical preservatives are no better for your dog than they are for you. A good red dye test is to place a small amount of canned or well-moistened dry food on a piece of white paper towel. Let the food sit there for about a half hour and then check to see if the towel has been stained. If the toweling has taken on a red stain, you can rest assured the color is there to appeal to your eye and not your dog's.

In nature the pack leader eats first. Your dog should be fed after you and your family eat.

Special Diets

A good number of dog-food manufacturers now produce special diets for overweight, underweight, and older dogs. While the amount of these foods that one should feed may remain the same as standard products, the calorie content is adjusted to suit the particular problem that accompanies each of these conditions.

There is no better remedy for these conditions, however, than using good, common sense. Obviously, too many calories and too little exercise will increase weight; fewer calories and an increase in physical activity reduces weight.

The geriatric or overweight dog needs a much lower-calorie diet than the growing puppy or adult dog of normal weight. It is also important to make sure your older dog get its fair share of exercise each day. The old-timer may prefer to spend more of its day on the sofa than when it was a youngster, but moderate exercise even for the very old dog will keep your friend alive much longer.

HOW-TO:
Teaching Commands

The Sit and Stay Commands

Equal in importance to the *No!* command and learning to come when called are the *Sit* and *Stay* commands. Even puppies can learn the *sit* command quickly, especially if it appears to be a game and a food treat is involved.

First, it is important to remember that the Australian cattle dog-in-training must be on collar and leash for this and all other lessons. This will avoid the possibility of the dog dashing off to avoid doing something it might not want to do at that moment.

Sit

Give the *Sit* command and immediately push down on the dog's hindquarters. Praise it

Give the sit *command and immediately push down on the dog's hindquarters.*

54

Once the sit lesson has been mastered, you can start on the stay *command.*

lavishly when it does sit, even though it is you who made the action take place. A food treat always seems to get the lesson across more quickly.

Continue holding your dog's rear end down, repeating the *Sit* command several times. If your dog makes an attempt to get up, repeat the command while exerting pressure on the rear end until the correct position is maintained. Make your dog stay in this position for increasing lengths of time; beginning with a few seconds and increasing the time as lessons progress over the following weeks.

Any attempt to get up or to lie down should be corrected by saying, *"No, Sit!"* in a firm voice. This should be accompanied by returning the dog to the desired *sit* position. Only when *you* decide your dog should get up should it be allowed to do so. When you do decide the dog can get up, call its name, say *"OK"* and make a big fuss over it. Praise and a food treat are in order every time your dog responds correctly.

Stay

Once the sit lesson has been mastered, start on the *stay* command. With your dog on leash and facing you, command it to sit. Take a step or two back and if your dog attempts to get up to follow you, say firmly, *"Sit, Stay!"* At the same time, raise your hand, palm toward the dog, and again command *"Stay!"*

Any attempt on your dog's part to get up must be corrected immediately, returning it to the sit position and repeating, *"Stay!"* Once your dog begins to understand what it must do, you can gradually increase the distance you step back from a few steps to several yards. Your Australian cattle dog eventually must learn that the *Sit, Stay* commands must be obeyed no matter how far away you are. Later, with advanced training, your dog will learn that the command is obeyed even when you move completely out of sight.

As your Australian cattle dog begins to understand what you want in this lesson, and has remained in the *sit* position for as long as you have dictated, do not make the mistake of calling it to you at first. This makes the dog overly anxious to get up and run to you. Instead, walk back to the dog and repeat the *"OK"* that is a signal the command is over. Later, when your dog becomes more reliable in this respect, you can call it to you.

The *Sit, Stay* lesson can take considerable time and patience with some dogs but usually the Australian cattle dog understands very quickly and, once understood, has little problem in demonstrating its newly acquired lesson.

With your dog sitting in front of you and facing you, give the command, down! *Then reach down and slide the dog's feet toward you.*

We reserve at least the *stay* part of the training until an Australian cattle dog is at least six months old because everything in a very young puppy's makeup dictates that, for protection, it get up and follow you wherever you go. Forcing a very young puppy to operate against its natural preservation instincts can be bewildering.

Down

Once your dog has mastered the *Sit* and *Stay* commands, you may begin work on *Down.* This is especially useful if you want your dog to remain in a particular place for a long period of time. *Down* is the one word command for *lie down. Down* must only be used when you want the dog to lie down. If you want your dog to get down from the sofa or to stop jumping on you, use the *off* command.

Early in the training there can be a little more resistance to obeying the *Down* command than there was to the *Sit* command. Once a dog has become accustomed to lying down on command, it seems to be more relaxing for the dog and it seems less inclined to get up and wander.

With your dog sitting in front of you and facing you, give the command, *Down!* Then reach down and slide the dog's front feet toward you. The dog will then automatically be lying down. Again, praise and a food treat are appropriate. Continue assisting your cattle dog into the *down* position until it does so on its own. Be firm and patient. Obeying this command can take a bit of time before some dogs respond, even when they understand fully what it is you want them to do.

Heel

Teaching your Australian cattle dog to heel is the very basis for off-leash control. In learning to heel, your dog will walk on your left side with its shoulder next to your leg no matter which direction you might go. We do not advocate ever having your dog off-leash when away from home, but it is reassuring to know that your dog will obey and stay with you regardless of circumstances. It should be easy to see how important a lesson this will be for safety's sake.

The Training Collar and Leash

I have found a lightweight, link-chain training collar to be very useful for all obedience training, particularly for the heeling lesson. It provides quick pressure around the neck and a snapping sound, both of which get the dog's attention. Erroneously referred to as a "choke collar," the link-chain collar used properly will not choke the dog.

As soon as your Australian cattle dog has learned to walk along on the leash, insist that it walk on your left side. A quick

A lightweight, link-chain training collar is ideal for obedience training, especially the heeling lesson.

short jerk on the leash will keep your dog from lunging from side to side, pulling ahead, or lagging back. Always keep the leash slack while your dog maintains the proper position at your side. Should the dog begin to drift away, give the *heel* command, followed immediately by a sharp jerk on the leash, and guide the dog back to the correct position.

Do not pull on the leash with steady pressure. All you need to get your dog's attention is a sharp but gentle jerking motion. It is amazing how quickly most Australian cattle dogs will learn to obey the *heel* command.

Teaching your dog to heel not only makes your walks more enjoyable, it is the very basis for off-leash control.

Bathing, Grooming, and Home Health Care

Equipment Needed

Your Australian cattle dog will not require much of your time or equipment in the way of grooming but that is not to say that it needs no care at all in this respect. While the Australian cattle dog's coat may be referred to as "wash and wear," regular brushing keeps the coat clean, odor-free and healthy. Most Australian cattle dogs will shed their coats twice a year. Brushing is an absolute necessity at this time particularly if your dog spends time indoors.

Regular grooming gives you the opportunity to keep on top of your dog's

Use a grooming table that has an "arm" and a "noose." This keeps the dog from fidgeting about or deciding that it has had enough grooming.

home health care needs. Such things as clipping nails, cleaning ears, and checking teeth can be taken care of during the time set aside for grooming.

Grooming table: Investing in a grooming table that has a non-slip top and an arm and noose can make all of these activities infinitely easier. These tables are available at pet shops and it is important to choose a table with a height that allows you to stand or sit comfortably while you are working on your dog. We use a grooming table that has an "arm" and a "noose." The noose slips around the dog's neck when it is standing and keeps the dog from fidgeting about or deciding it has had enough grooming.

Do not attempt to groom or attend to your dog's health care while you and your dog are sitting on the floor. You will spend most of your time chasing the dog around the room and Australian cattle dogs, particularly, will simply wander off when they feel they have had enough of your attention.

Brushes, combs, clippers: Invest in a good stiff bristle or wire brush, a steel comb, and animal nail clippers. You will be using this equipment for many years so buy the best equipment that you can afford.

Brushing

Undoubtedly, the breeder from whom you purchased your Australian cattle dog will have begun to accustom the puppy to grooming just as soon as there was enough hair to brush. You must continue with grooming sessions or begin them at once if for some reason they have not been started. It is imperative that you both learn to cooperate in this endeavor in order to make it an easy and pleasant experience.

Brush with the lay of the hair and use the steel comb on the longer hair of the "pants" on the dog's rear legs and on the tail. At shedding time there will be a tremendous amount of hair collected in your brush and comb. You can hasten this process by giving your cattle dog a warm bath once the shedding has begun. This loosens the hair and, though you may think your dog will complete the process completely bald, fear not—once the dead coat has been removed, the shedding stops and new hair growth will begin.

Nail Trimming and Foot Care

This is a good time to accustom your Australian cattle dog to having its nails trimmed and having its feet inspected. Always inspect your dog's feet for cracked pads. Check between the toes for splinters and thorns, paying particular attention to any swollen or tender areas. In many sections of the country there is a weed that has a barbed hooklike affair that carries its seed. This hook easily finds its way into a dog's foot or between its toes and very quickly works its way deep into the dog's flesh, causing soreness

Necessary Grooming Equipment
- grooming table
- stiff bristle or wire brush
- steel comb
- nail clippers
- scissors
- rubber mat
- spray hose
- cotton balls
- shampoo
- washcloth
- heavy towels

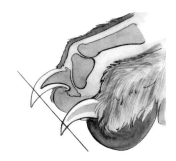

Each of the dog's nails has a blood vessel running through the center called the "quick." The quick grows close to the end of the nail and contains very sensitive nerve endings.

and infection. These barbs are best removed by your veterinarian before serious problems result.

We suggest attending to your dog's nails every other week. The nails of an Australian cattle dog that spends most of its time indoors or on grass when outdoors can grow long very quickly. Do not allow the nails to become overgrown and then expect to cut them back easily. Each nail has a blood vessel running through the center called the "quick." The quick grows close to the end of the nail and contains very sensitive nerve endings. If the nail is allowed to grow too long it will be impossible to cut it back to a proper length without cutting into the quick. This causes severe pain to the dog and can also result in a great deal of bleeding that can be very difficult to stop.

If your cattle dog is getting plenty of exercise on cement or rough hard pavement, the nails may stay sufficiently worn down; otherwise, the nails can grow long very quickly. They must then be trimmed with canine nail clippers, an electric nail grinder (also called a drummel), or coarse file made expressly for that purpose.

The Australian cattle dog's dark nails make it practically impossible to see where the quick ends, so

It is important to train your Australian cattle dog that it must behave while you cut its nails.

regardless of which nail trimming device is used, you must proceed with caution and remove only a small portion of the nail at a time.

Should the quick be nipped in the trimming process, there are any number of blood-clotting products available at pet shops that will almost immediately stem the flow of blood. It is wise to have one of these products on hand in case your dog breaks a nail in some way.

Bathing

Dog show exhibitors use coat care products that adhere to the cattle dog's hair and most exhibitors bathe their dogs before shows. Even at that, some exhibitors do use "dry bath" products rather than the tub and shampoo method. Well-kept Australian cattle dogs are literally odor-free and frequent bathing is unnecessary.

When your cattle dog does require a wet bath, you will need to gather the necessary equipment ahead of time. A rubber mat should be placed at the bottom of the tub to keep your dog from slipping and thereby becoming frightened. A rubber spray hose is absolutely necessary to thoroughly wet the coat. It is also necessary to remove all shampoo residue.

A small cotton ball placed inside each ear will prevent water from running down into the dog's ear canal. Be very careful when washing around the eyes as soaps and shampoos can be extremely irritating.

It is best to use a shampoo designed especially for dogs; the pH balance is adjusted to keep drying to a minimum and leaves the hair shining and lustrous.

Technique

In bathing, start behind the ears and work back. Use a washcloth to apply the soap, and rinse around the head and face. Once you have shampooed your dog, you must rinse the coat thoroughly and when you feel quite certain all shampoo residue has been removed, rinse once more. Shampoo residue in the coat is sure to dry the hair and could cause skin irritation.

As soon as you have completed the bath, use heavy towels to remove as much of the excess water as possible. Your dog will assist you in the process by shaking a great deal of the water out of its coat on its own.

Home Health Care

It is important to establish a weekly health care routine for your Australian cattle dog. Maintaining this schedule will prevent escalation of serious problems that may take expensive veterinary attention.

Eye care: If the eyes are inflamed or discharging any kind of matter, check for foreign bodies such as soot or weed seeds. Regular flushing of the eye with cotton and cool water will help relieve the eye of debris and pollen. If your dog's eyes water continuously, have your veterinarian inspect them for a condition called entropion, in which the eyelid is inverted and the eyelashes cause irritation to the eye. It can be corrected by surgery. Entropion is very rare in

Australian cattle dogs but has been reported in some instances.

Ear cleaning: The insides of the ears should always be clean and pink. Nothing other than a cotton Q-tip should ever be inserted into the ear itself and never probe into the inner recess of the ear. Use the Q-tip moistened with olive or almond oil to clean the ear. If wax has accumulated, dip the Q-tip into rubbing alcohol, squeeze out the excess thoroughly, and clean out the ear.

Do not attempt to treat an ear that has an unpleasant odor. Consult your veterinarian immediately. The odor may indicate the presence of parasites in the ear or worse, there may be an ear infection.

Anal sacs: The anal sacs (also referred to as the anal *glands* by many breeders) are located on each side of the anus and should be regularly looked after. They can become blocked, causing extreme irritation and abscesses in advanced cases.

If you notice your Australian cattle dog pulling itself along the ground when it is sitting down, you should check the anal glands. While not a particularly pleasant part of keeping your dog healthy, if regularly attended to, keeping the anal glands clear is relatively easy.

The best time to attend to this job is when you are giving your dog its bath. With the dog in the tub, place your thumb and forefinger of one hand on either side of the anal passage and exert pressure. The glands will empty quickly. Wear rubber gloves when performing this function and it is best to cover the anus itself with a cotton swab or tissue. Should you be unsure of how to perform this procedure, your veterinarian or the breeder from whom you purchased your Australian cattle dog will instruct you.

Dental care: Care should always be given to the state of your dog's teeth.

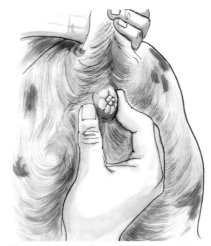

Emptying the anal glands is important to your dog's health. Pressure on on either side of the anal passage will empty the glands quickly.

If your dog has been accustomed to chewing hard dog biscuits or gnawing on large rawhide bones since puppy-hood, it is unlikely that you will have any problems as this chewing activity assists greatly in removing dental plaque, which is the major cause of tooth decay. Any sign of redness of the gums or tooth decay merits expert attention.

Retention of baby teeth can cause long-term problems with the permanent teeth. Generally, by the time the permanent teeth have come through at about five months of age, the baby teeth have all fallen out. If there are any baby teeth remaining at this stage, seek your veterinarian's advice on their removal. Retaining baby teeth can interfere with the proper placement of your Australian cattle dog's permanent teeth.

Parasites

Fleas: While fleas are a problem everywhere, these pests can be especially troublesome for those who live

As fastidious as you might be about caring for your cattle dog and keeping the coat in good condition, you must be aware that fleas lurk everywhere and are a problem to deal with.

If you find fleas—even one flea—on your dog, there are undoubtedly hundreds of others lurking in the carpeting and furniture just waiting for your dog to emerge from the tub so that they can hop back on.

The only way to combat fleas is to rid dog, house, and yard of the problem all at the same time. Simultaneously with your dog's flea bath, you must eliminate fleas from within your home and surrounding outdoor premises.

Flea bombs manufactured for this purpose are available at most hardware stores and veterinary offices. If your Australian cattle dog, like most dogs, spends any time at all in your yard or garden, you must also spray that area with one of the many products available at pet shops and hardware stores.

The most efficient way to eliminate the flea problem is to arrange for your cattle dog to have a flea bath at the local dog-grooming salon. Make an appointment to have a commercial pest control service come to your home while your dog is at the groomer. The service will spray both the interior of your home and the surrounding property as well. Most of these companies guarantee their work for a specific period of time and many offer a monthly or quarterly plan by which they will return to make sure the problem does not get out of hand again.

Flea collars: The latest advance in flea collars is one that emits an artificial hormone that inhibits the development of any larva that can be deposited on your dog by a live flea. This must be accompanied by a complete and repeated flea elimination program in the household and surrounding area.

Lack of success in the use of the bathing and collar methods described is more apt to be the result of not fol-

in climates that have no freezing temperatures to kill off the existing infestation. Granted, the flea force returns just as soon as the warmer weather sets in, but there is at least some respite. The more temperate climates do not even have this relief.

As fastidious as you might be about caring for your Australian cattle dog and keeping its coat in good condition, you must be aware that fleas will still be a problem. Even if you were to protect your cattle dog like a hot house flower, its daily walks can bring fleas into your home and once there, the little creatures multiply with alarming rapidity.

Dips and sprays: Bathing or "dipping" your Australian cattle dog with a good flea soap or product manufactured to eliminate fleas is not enough.

lowing product instructions. There is also the possibility of toxicity when using flea sprays or flea collars. It is very important to read instructions on the packaging of these items very carefully.

Flea pills: A pill has been developed that, administered orally once a month, conditions, the dog's system to totally interfere with the maturation of eggs and larval fleas and prevents them from becoming normal, reproducing adults. After biting the dog, the flea passes on the inhibitor to its offspring.

The pill does not eliminate mature fleas. Sprays and soaps must still be used to eliminate the existing adult fleas, but a combination of prescribed pill use and local applications of flea products can eventually eliminate the problem.

Nature's way: Many people dislike using chemical toxins of any kind on or around themselves or their dogs. A number of natural products are in use that reportedly are effective in flea control and elimination.

When ingested by a dog, brewer's yeast gives an odor that repels fleas. Citronella is another product that has an odor that fleas dislike. Other products made from citrus oils are said to paralyze the flea's respiratory system.

It is always best to consult a veterinarian for help in fighting the flea battle. He or she knows which products are most effective in the immediate area and they are inclined to keep abreast of new developments in combating the problem.

Fleas act as carriers of the tapeworm's eggs. When a dog swallows a flea, the tapeworm eggs grow in the dog's intestines. Tapeworms are discussed under the heading Internal Parasites on page 67.

Lice: Lice are seldom a problem with the well-cared for Australian cattle dog, because the pests are

Even healthy puppies like this should see their veterinarian for regular check-ups.

spread by direct contact. In other words, to have lice your dog must spend time with another animal that has lice or be groomed with a contaminated brush or comb. Since these pests are minute in size, they are not as easy to see as fleas.

If no fleas are present and you suspect lice, the dog must be bathed with an insecticidal shampoo every week until the problem is eliminated. Fortunately, unlike fleas, lice live and breed entirely on the dog, so it is not necessary to treat the entire area in which the dog lives.

Ear mites: Ear mites are parasites that settle in the external ear canal. They can lead to chronic irritation. Symptoms are an extremely disagreeable odor, a dark waxy secretion, and constant scratching at the ear by the

61

dog. Once present, ear mites can be extremely persistent, particularly if a dog becomes severely infested. Flushing of the ear by a veterinarian is recommended.

Ticks: Your cattle dog can pick up ticks by running through grass, wooded areas, or even through sand at the beach. Ticks are bloodsucking insects that bury their heads firmly into the skin. They can become a source of extreme irritation to your dog and can cause secondary infections as well. It is important to loosen the tick's grip before you attempt to remove it; otherwise, you may allow the head to break away from the tick and remain lodged in the dog's skin. This also can create severe infections.

To remove adult ticks, soak them with a spray made especially for tick removal; once the parasite has loosened its grip, you can remove it with a pair of tweezers. Regular bathing with a tick dip will prevent reinfestation, but, as is the case with all dips and sprays, read the instructions carefully as some of these products may be toxic.

The entire environment in which the dog lives must be regularly and vigorously treated against ticks especially if you live adjacent to a wooded area or beach. Ticks can transmit serious diseases that can endanger humans as well as animals. In some areas ticks carry Lyme disease and Rocky Mountain spotted fever. It is important that you discuss the tick problem with your local veterinarian, who can advise you on which dangers might present themselves.

Vomiting and diarrhea

Perhaps the most common canine ailments are vomiting and diarrhea. They do not indicate that your dog is seriously ill, but should either symptom persist for more than 24 hours, do not hesitate to call your veterinarian. Young puppies should be seen sooner as they can quickly dehydrate.

Evidence of blood, either "coffee ground" in appearance in vomit or black and tarlike in stools, warrants an immediate visit to your veterinarian.

Dogs may vomit to purge their digestive tracts. Puppies may do so when they eat too much or too fast. Intense exercise directly after eating can cause vomiting. None of this is cause for alarm unless it occurs repeatedly.

For occasional diarrhea, change from your dog's regular diet to thoroughly cooked rice with a small amount of boiled chicken added. Maintain this kind of diet until the condition improves and then gradually return your dog to its normal diet.

Medical Problems

Minor accidents and illnesses will undoubtedly occur while your Australian cattle dog progresses through puppyhood, adolescence, and on into old age. This chapter is written in the hope that it will assist the owner of a pet Australian cattle dog to determine the difference between situations that can easily be taken care of at home and those that demand veterinary treatment.

There is one piece of advice that always applies: If you are in doubt about the seriousness of your dog's problem, do not hesitate to pick up the phone and call your veterinarian; he or she knows which questions to ask and will be able to determine whether or not it is necessary to see your dog.

Immunizations

Very effective vaccines have been developed to combat diseases that once were fatal to practically any infected dog. The danger of an Australian cattle dog being infected with distemper, hepatitis, leptospirosis, or the extremely virulent parvovirus is highly unlikely if proper inoculations and booster shots have been given regularly. Rabies among well cared-for dogs is practically unheard of, but dogs that come in contact with animals in nature can be at risk if not immunized. Your veterinarian may also recommend immunizations against kennel cough and coronavirus.

Immunization against these infectious diseases begins in puppyhood and it is extremely important that you follow your veterinarian's inoculation schedule; neglecting to do so could easily cost your dog's life. On occasion, however, there are dogs that, for one reason or another, do not develop full immunity. Any marked change in your dog's behavior should be observed very closely, especially if your dog is under a year of age.

Should your dog suddenly become listless, refuse food, and start to cough and sneeze, contact your veterinarian at once. Other signs of possible problems in this area are marked increase in thirst, blood in the stools or urine, and discharge of any kind from the nose.

Emergencies

Accidents

Injuries sustained in a road accident can be fatal if not handled correctly and promptly. If your dog is struck by an automobile or motorcycle, it is important that you remain calm. Panic on your part will serve only to upset the injured animal and could cause it to thrash around and injure itself even more seriously.

Often an injured animal is panicky and may snap at you. Muzzle the dog before lifting it to prevent any injury to yourself.

If your dog is unable to move itself, immediately remove it from the street where it could be further injured. In picking up your injured dog, it is critical that you support the body as fully as possible. The less movement of the injured area the better.

Very effective vaccines have been developed to combat canine infectious diseases.

63

Any marked change in your dog's behavior should be observed very closely, especially if your dog is under a year of age.

The Australian cattle dog is of a size that the average person can lift and support the dog without too much difficulty. If for some reason you are alone and lifting your dog presents a problem, gently place it on a blanket and carefully slide the blanket to the vehicle that you will use to transport the dog to your veterinarian.

Do not wait to determine the extent of injury. Internal injuries may have occurred that you are unable to observe immediately. Get the injured dog to a veterinarian without delay. Ask someone to drive you there so that you are free to hold your injured dog and keep it calm. If there is no one else available to drive you, put the injured dog in a box or shipping kennel of some kind to keep it as immobile as possible.

Bleeding Wounds

If there is a bleeding wound due to a traffic accident or any other accident, deal with the bleeding at once. Using a pad of cotton or a compress soaked in cold water, apply pressure directly to the bleeding point. If the flow of blood is not stemmed, your dog could bleed to death.

An Australian cattle dog seldom will pick fights with other dogs, but they are not inclined to back down when challenged. Should your dog be injured in a fight, get it to the veterinarian without delay. Bite wounds are invariably infected and antibiotic treatment is necessary.

Stings and Bites

Australian cattle dogs are curious animals and seem fascinated by all things that fly and crawl. They naturally attempt to examine insects with their paws or mouths. This can lead to bites and stings on the foot, or worse, on or around the mouth or nose.

If the stinger is visible, remove it with a pair of tweezers and apply a saline solution or mild antiseptic. If the swelling is large, particularly inside the mouth, or if the dog appears to be in shock, contact your veterinarian at once.

When to Call Your Veterinarian
- Persistent coughing or sneezing
- Gasping for breath
- Vomiting
- Diarrhea
- Continued listlessness
- Loss of appetite
- Excessive thirst
- Runny nose
- Discharge from the eyes or ears
- Blood in the stool
- Limping, trembling, or shaking
- Abscesses, lumps, or swellings
- Dark or cloudy urine
- Difficult urination
- Loss of bowel or bladder control
- Deep red or white gums

Foreign Objects

Should you see your Australian cattle dog pawing at its mouth or rubbing its mouth along the ground, immediately check to see if there is something lodged in the dog's mouth. Australian cattle dogs can shatter bones and objects that most other dogs would be incapable of doing and can manage to get the object lodged or trapped across their teeth, usually halfway back, or even at the back of the mouth where the two jaws hinge.

Should this be the case, grasp the object firmly between your fingers and push firmly toward the back of the mouth where the teeth are wider. This will usually dislodge the object, but be sure to have a firm grip on the object so the dog does not swallow it. If you are unable to remove the object quickly, get the dog to the veterinarian at once.

If you suspect your dog has swallowed a small ball or some other object, check to see if the object is visible in the dog's throat. If so, reach in, grasp the object firmly, and pull it out. If the dog seems to be experiencing difficulty in breathing, the object may be lodged in the windpipe. Sharp

Australian cattle dogs are innately curious. If any small object is missing in the home and you suspect your dog may have ingested it, do not hesitate to consult your veterinarian. An X-ray will reveal the hidden "treasure" and save your dog's life.

If Your Australian Cattle Dog Is Poisoned

Be prepared in the event that your cattle dog is poisoned:

1. Keep the telephone number of your local poison control center with your other emergency numbers.

2. If you know or suspect which poison your dog has ingested, give this information to the poison control center when you call them. They may be able to prescribe an immediate antidote.

3. Have the emergency number of your dog's veterinarian or the nearest 24-hour emergency veterinary hospital current and easily available. Give any information you receive

from the poison control center to your veterinarian.

4. If you are not sure that your dog has been poisoned or which poison it may have ingested, describe the symptoms you are observing to your veterinarian.

5. Common symptoms of poisoning:
- Convulsions
- Paralysis
- Tremors
- Vomiting
- Diarrhea
- Stomach cramps and pains, accompanied by whimpering or howling, heavy breathing.

blows to the rib cage may cause the dog to expel air from the lungs and also expel the object.

If any small object is missing in the home and you suspect your dog may have ingested it, do not hesitate to consult your veterinarian. An X-ray will reveal the hidden "treasure" and save your dog's life.

Illnesses

Rabies

It is important that you are aware of the clinical signs of rabies in animals and report any animal bites to your veterinarian. Generally speaking, there are two types of rabies: the violent type and what is referred to as the dumb type. In the violent type the afflicted animal goes wild, biting and attacking anything that moves. An animal with the dumb type of rabies will appear to be paralyzed and may sit staring without focus. The animal's lower jaw may hang open, emitting saliva.

Life cycle of the tapeworm: fleas are commonly hosts of the tapeworm. When the flea is swallowed, the parasite is shared with your dog—tapeworms develop and segments are passed in the feces.

Rabies shots are normally given when puppies are four to six months old. Again, the possibility of your cattle dog coming into contact with undomesticated animals may make earlier immunization a wise choice, and you should discuss this with your veterinarian.

Kennel Cough

Kennel cough (infectious rhinotracheitis), while highly infectious, is not a serious disease; it is like a mild case of influenza in humans. It is caused by a mixture of a bacteria and a virus. The name of the disease is misleading as it implies that a dog must be in a kennel environment to be infected. Actually, it is very easily passed from one dog to another in almost any situation.

The symptoms can make the disease sound far worse than it actually is. They are particularly nerve-wracking because there is a persistent hacking cough that at times makes one think that surely the dog will bring up everything it has ever eaten!

There are various protective procedures now available that can be administered by your veterinarian. In addition to inoculations, there is an intranasal vaccine available. These protective measures are advisable for your Australian cattle dog if you ever take it to a dog park or plan on placing it in a boarding kennel. Many boarding kennels now insist upon proof of protection against kennel cough before they will allow a dog to be admitted.

Coronavirus

Coronavirus, also referred to as coronaviral gastroenteritis, is a highly contagious virus and can be caused by ingesting fecal matter of an infected canid, which can also include coyotes and foxes. Dogs of any age can be infected and symptoms include watery stools, vomiting, and anorexia. Coronavirus can be successfully treated by a veterinarian but immunization is recommended to prevent the disease.

Internal Parasites

Tapeworms and heartworms are best diagnosed and treated by your veterinarian. Great advances are continually made in dealing with both of these parasites and what was once a complicated and time-consuming treatment has been simplified over the years. Most of the dog's internal parasites are readily detected by your veterinarian's microscopic inspection of the dog's stool.

Tapeworms: Tapeworms are a part of the life cycle of the flea. If your dog has now or has had fleas in the past, it undoubtedly has tapeworm. A sign of infection is the appearance of segments of the worm crawling around the dog's anus or in the stool just after the dog has relieved itself. Your veterinarian can inoculate your Australian cattle dog if it has this problem, and the tapeworms are quickly and completely eliminated.

Whipworms: Whipworms are round and tapered in shape. These parasites normally settle in the cecum and upper part of the large intestine. They are extremely difficult to see other than by veterinary inspection of the stool. The parasites thrive on the host and can cause severe impairment of the dog's health and, in extreme cases, even death.

Roundworms: Roundworms are not an unusual condition in dogs and are rarely harmful in an adult dog; however, these parasites can cause extreme health hazards to puppies if present in large amounts.

Roundworms can be transmitted from mother to puppies so make sure that your female is free of roundworms before you breed her if you plan on a litter of puppies.

Hookworms: These tiny parasites attach themselves to the insides of the

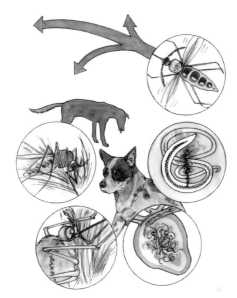

Life cycle of the heartworm: infected mosquitoes bite your dog and deposit the heartworm larvae on its skin. The larvae enter the bloodstream through the hole created by the mosquito bite and make their way to the dog's heart.

small intestines. They multiply rapidly and suck the blood of the infected dog. This can be extremely and quickly debilitating to puppies and young dogs. Stool sample examination by a veterinarian is recommended for any dog or puppy that continues to act listless.

Heartworms: Heartworms are parasitic worms found in dogs' hearts. Dogs are the only mammals that are commonly affected. The worm is transmitted by mosquitoes that carry the larvae of the worm.

Your veterinarian can detect the presence of heartworm by a blood test. There are preventive medications for a dog that tests negative for heartworms and corrective measures for the dog that has been infected.

Inherited Health Problems and Diseases

Like all breeds of domesticated dogs, the Australian cattle dog has its share of hereditary problems; fortunately, the problems are relatively few. Some fanciers are inclined to believe this is due to the proximity of the breed's dingo heritage. The dingo is free of incapacitating problems due to a process called natural selection. Any genetically transferred infirmity that would interfere with a wild dog's ability to nurse as a puppy, to capture food as an adult, or to escape from a predator, would automatically eliminate the individual from the gene pool.

We who control the breeding of our domesticated dogs are intent upon saving all the puppies in a litter, but in preserving life we also perpetuate health problems. Our humanitarian proclivities thus have a downside as well.

The diseases described here may not be present in the Australian cattle dog you buy, nor are these problems necessarily to be found in your Australian cattle dog's immediate ancestors. They are breed problems, however, that should be discussed with the breeder from whom you purchase your dog. As stated previously, the reputable Australian cattle dog breeder is aware of the following problems and should be more than willing to discuss them with you.

Deafness

The most serious congenital defect of the Australian cattle dog is deafness. This problem exists in collies, bull terriers, and Dalmatians, all three of which are known to have been used in the development of the Australian cattle dog.

It is extremely difficult to detect this problem when puppies are young, particularly while a puppy is still living with its littermates. An afflicted puppy is apt to respond in the same manner as it sees its littermates respond to a noise or situation.

Experienced breeders are aware that puppies can be tested for the problem even as early as five weeks old by using what is called the BAER (Brainstem Auditory Evoked Response) Test. Needless to say, a deaf dog makes a poor choice as a companion and afflicted animals should never be bred.

Hip Dysplasia

Hip dysplasia is a developmental disease of the hip joint. The result is instability of the hip joint due to abnormal contours of one or both of the hip joints. Some dogs might show tenderness in the hip, walk with a limp or swaying gait, or experience difficulty getting up. Symptoms vary from mild temporary lameness to severe crippling in extreme cases. Treatment may require surgery. The problem is not rampant in the Australian cattle dog as a breed but enough cases have been reported to merit discussing it with any breeder you might consider buying a puppy from.

Progressive Retinal Atrophy

Progressive retinal atrophy, commonly referred to as "PRA," is a degenerative disease of the retinal cells of the eye that progresses to blindness. It usually occurs later in a Australian cattle dog's life—beyond the age of six years. Eye testing of breeding stock is now done by responsible breeders, which is a fortunate situation. Detecting the "carriers" of PRA and avoiding their use in a breeding program can all but eliminate the problem entirely.

Sharing Your Life with an Australian Cattle Dog

Enjoying the Breed's Versatility

Everything in the Australian cattle dog's history and genetic makeup tells the same story—this is a working dog. If prospective dog owners are looking for a companion that loves to sit on its owner's lap all day or one that is content to lie patiently in front of the hearth while its owners are away, they should *not* consider an Australian cattle dog!

The Australian cattle dog's heritage equips it to work all day in blistering sun or freezing winds. It innately knows what to do and how to do it. Do not expect an Australian cattle dog to harness that physical and psychic energy and keep it in reserve until its owner is ready for a restrained walk around the block.

There is no such thing as a cattle dog that has nothing to do. If a cattle dog's owner does not provide the dog with assigned duties, the dog will create its own activity schedule and, rest assured, more often than not the activities involved will seldom please the owner!

On the other hand, if the prospective owner of an Australian cattle dog is an active person who also derives as much pleasure from training a dog as this breed derives from being trained, this person will undoubtedly join the ranks of the thousands of cattle dog owners who consider the breed one of the most trainable and intelligent in existence.

Range of Activities

If an activity calls for speed, endurance, athletic ability, and intelligence, the Australian cattle dog is a great candidate. There is such a wide array of events an Australian cattle dog is capable of competing (and excelling) in that it is highly unlikely that even the owner whose energy and athletic ability registers at decathlon level will ever exhaust the cattle dog's potential.

What makes an Australian cattle dog such a versatile breed is its ability to perform well in a wide array of activities with complete ease. Your cattle

The Australian cattle dog lives for that moment its owner says, "OK, let's go!"

dog can be a Canine Good Citizen certificate holder, conformation show competitor, obedience trial star, speed demon on the agility course, herding trial whiz and Schutzhund candidate—and this is just scratching the surface of activities in which the Australian cattle dog can participate.

On a more serious note the Australian cattle dog's great scenting ability makes it a perfect candidate for drug and explosive detection as well as search-and-rescue work. Australian cattle dogs are also proving they can also make wonderful therapy dogs for the aged and infirmed.

Companions

The wonderful thing about all this is that the more involved and the more proficient your Australian cattle dog becomes in any or for that matter *all* of the above, the better it will become at being your best buddy and companion! While we have said time and time again that the Australian cattle dog is not a dog for everyone, we can also say the owner who is suited to this breed could not possibly hope to have a better dog.

It would be impossible to give all the detailed training instructions necessary to make your Australian cattle dog proficient in the many activities for which it is suitable. We will, however, endeavor to give a broad overview of the activities that many cattle dogs have excelled in and leave it up to the owners to pursue any of them in which they have an interest. Additional information on these activities can be found in the chapter on Useful Addresses and Literature, beginning on page 93.

Conformation Shows

Popular and well-attended dog events are the combined conformation shows and obedience trials that are regulated by the American Kennel Club and the United Kennel Club. The origi-

nal purpose of conformation shows was to give breeders a means of comparing their stock to that of other fanciers and thereby make improvements in their breeding programs.

Today, not all people who participate in conformation shows intend to become breeders. Many simply find enjoyment in the competitive aspect of these events. Referred to by some as "canine beauty contests," conformation dog shows take place nearly every weekend of the year in one part of the country or another and are open to all non-neutered, AKC and UKC-registered dogs.

Generally speaking, conformation shows fall into two major categories: matches and championship events. Match shows are primarily staged for the young or inexperienced dogs that are not ready to compete for championship points. In most cases, classes are offered for dogs from about three months of age and older.

Match Shows

Matches are an excellent place for novice handlers to learn to show their own dogs. Since these match shows are far more informal than championship events, there is plenty of time for the novice handler to ask questions and seek assistance from more experienced exhibitors or from the officiating judges.

Match shows can be held for all breeds or they can be what are referred to as "specialty matches," which are for one particular breed of dog. When there is a club devoted to a specific breed in an area, that club will often hold these match shows so that the newer club members and the young puppies will have an opportunity to gain some experience.

Information regarding these matches can usually be found in the classified sections of Sunday newspapers under "Dogs for Sale." Local breeders are usually aware of upcoming events of this kind as well.

There is no need to enter these informal matches ahead of time. Most accept entries on the grounds of the show site the morning of the event. The person taking your entry will be able to assist you in filling out the entry form and give you the preliminary instructions you will need.

Championship Shows

Championship shows are much more formal in nature and best entered after you have gained some experience by participating in several match events. Championship shows are sponsored by various all-breed kennel clubs or in some instances by a club specializing in one particular breed of dog. The AKC and the UKC can provide you with the name of the all-breed kennel club in your area and the Australian Cattle Dog Club of America can let you know if there is an Australian cattle dog specialty club in your vicinity (see Useful Addresses and Literature, page 93).

How a Champion Is Made

A registered dog can become a champion of record by winning a given number of championship "points." These points are awarded to the best male and best female nonchampions in each breed. The number of championship points that can be won at a particular show is based upon the number of entries in a dog's own breed and sex entered at the show and the area in which the show is located. These requirements are determined by the organization sponsoring the event, primarily the AKC or UKC.

Catalogs sold at all championship shows list the particulars relevant to every dog entered in the show. The catalog also lists the number of dogs required in each breed to win from one through five points. Since the number of dogs necessary for the various number of points differs geographically, it is important to check the catalog at each show you attend at which your male or female has been awarded points.

Canine Good Citizen Test

Though this event does not achieve any official title, it is nonetheless an extremely valuable accomplishment. The purpose of the test is to demonstrate that the canine entered is well mannered and an asset to the community. There are ten parts to the test and the dog must pass all ten in order to be awarded a certificate:

1. Appearance and grooming
2. Acceptance of a stranger
3. Walking on a loose leash; heel and execute turns and halts.
4. Walking through a crowd
5. Sitting for examination
6. Sitting and lying down on command
7. Staying in both the *sit* and *down* position
8. Positive reaction to another dog
9. Calm reaction to distracting sights or noises
10. Ability to be left alone (tied with leash while owner is out of sight)

Trials and Events

Obedience

Obedience trials are held at both championship shows and matches, as are the conformation events. The same informal entry procedures that apply to conformation matches apply here as well. The championship or "sanctioned" obedience trials are normally held in conjunction with conformation events and normally require pre-entry.

Obedience training classes are definitely prerequisites here, since competition is highly precise and based entirely upon your dog's performing a set series of exercises. The exercises required in the various classes of

The Australian cattle dog has proven over and over that it can be a star at conformation dog shows and obedience trials. Many cattle dogs win at both events on the same day.

competition range from basics like *heel, sit,* and *lie down* in the novice class on through the sophisticated exercises of the utility and tracking dog levels that require scent discrimination and directed jumping.

Each level has a degree that can be earned after attaining qualifying scores at a given number of shows. The com-

This Australian cattle dog is not only a conformation show champion but an accomplished tracking dog as well. This dog acquired his tracking dog title at the tender age of seven months.

petition levels and corresponding degrees are: Novice earning a Companion Dog degree (CD), Open that earns the Companion Dog Excellent degree (CDX), and Utility earning the Utility Dog and Utility Dog Excellent degrees (UD and UDX). Tracking events earn the rare Tracking Dog and Tracking Dog Excellent titles (TD and TDX).

Agility

Agility competition is actually an obstacle course for dogs. Everyone involved (and everyone who watches) appears to be having the time of their lives. There are 14 obstacles that the canine contestants must master off-leash while being timed. The course includes tunnels, cat walks, seesaws, hoops, and numerous other obstacles. Still in the early stages of growth, this event is catching on rapidly and will undoubtedly become one of the biggest attractions at all breed dog shows.

Herding Tests and Trials

It goes without saying that herding trials employ the very essence of the Australian cattle dog. Australian cattle dog breeders encourage every owner of the breed to participate in these events as the trials preserve and perpetuate the breed's celebrated herding instincts.

Herding trials are sponsored by the AKC and are open to dogs over nine months of age that are registered with the organization as a herding breed. There are three levels of competition involved in the AKC's program: Herding Tested, Pre-trial Testing, and Herding Trials.

Herding test: This test is quite simple as it is designed to reveal the dog's willingness to respond to its handler and its ability to control the movement of the livestock involved— cattle, goats, sheep, or even ducks.

In order to pass the test the dog must successfully accomplish the following:

1. Execute a *stay* on command.
2. Follow two commands to change the direction of the moving stock.
3. Stop on command.
4. Come on recall.

Ten minutes are allowed for the exercises. The dog must successfully pass two such tests under two different judges and no score is given; the test is either passed or failed. After passing both tests, the participating dog is awarded the Herding Tested (HT) degree, which becomes an official title and can be added to its registered name.

Pre-trial test: Once earned, the HT degree makes the dog eligible for the Pre-trial test. In this event the dog must:
1. Work the livestock through obstacles.
2. Stop the stock.
3. Turn the stock.
4. Reverse the direction of the stock.
5. Pen the stock within ten minutes.

This is also a pass or fail event that must be successfully completed under two different judges and earns the official Pre-trial Tested (PT) title.

Herding trial: Dogs competing in the Herding Trial events have three options in which to compete designated as the A, B or C courses. The three courses are designed to show different areas of working ability.

Each of the courses has three levels of accomplishment: Herding Started (HS), Herding Intermediate (HI), and Advanced. Proficiency in the Advanced level earns the dog a Herding Excellent (HX) title that is the highest degree attainable by a herding dog.

All of these trials must be completed with a score of at least 60 out of a possible 100 points, which are divided into six categories of proficiency. A dog must earn at least half of the points allotted to each of the six categories in order to qualify.

The courses involve complex patterns, many of which require a partic-

The final exercise in the pre-trial test is to drive the cattle into a holding pen.

ipating dog to respond to hand signals from the handler rather than to verbal commands. Details of these complex trials can be obtained from the AKC's Herding Department and there are numerous books and periodicals on the subject listed in the last chapter of this book. The AKC also sponsors herding trial clinics at various locations throughout the United States though the year.

Schutzhund

The purpose of Schutzhund training is to test a dog's ability in the area of obedience, tracking, and protection. There are three levels of proficiency (Schutzhund I, II, and III) in each of the three parts and a dog is tested in all three parts at the same trial. A passing score is required in each of the three parts in order to acquire the Schutzhund degree.

It is very important to understand that the purpose of Schutzhund training is to develop a well-adjusted and well-trained dog friendly to all who have no hostile intentions. A Schutzhund dog is *not* an attack dog; it performs on command—and only on command—and is not a loose cannon exploding at will. Schutzhund training is not to be taken lightly nor undertaken without qualified supervision.

Fun and Games

Your Australian cattle dog will play games far longer than you may want to, but it is certainly a way in which you can both stay fit and you can help release some of your dog's stored-up energy.

Frisbee: An Australian cattle dog will retrieve a frisbee for hours on end and the breed is especially adept at learning how to catch the thrown frisbee. There are competitions and even national championships offered for dogs excelling in the sport.

Flyball: Flyball is a race in which two teams of four dogs race over hurdles to trigger a box that releases a ball that they carry back over the hurdles. The Australian cattle dog is a star at this event.

Hiking: The dedicated outdoors man or woman could not possibly have a better companion than the Australian cattle dog. The breed will enjoy hiking as much as any human and its human companion does not have the worry of the cattle dog wandering off and disappearing for hours on end; the cattle dog wants to be with its owner—*always.*

Swimming: If the Australian cattle dog owner enjoys a day at the beach or in the surf, the Australian cattle dog

The Australian cattle dog loves games that include retrieving. Playing frisbee can keep a cattle dog interested for hours.

The Australian cattle dog loves water and can be an expert swimmer.

The cattle dog is a star at playing flyball.

will also be right there. The breed loves water and is an excellent swimmer. Owners who live near a lake or pond find that their cattle dogs will usually take several swimming breaks a day when temperatures rise.

While we caution prospective dog owners that the Australian cattle dog is not a breed for everyone, those who are suited to the breed are to be envied. They couldn't have a better canine friend and companion.

Breeding

Factors to Consider

As mentioned previously, there is a serious pet overpopulation problem in the United States; therefore, an Australian cattle dog owner should think long and hard before making yet another contribution to this critical situation. Admiration of the unique qualities of the Australian cattle dog is undoubtedly what inspires an owner to consider breeding, but one must stop to realize that the breed is not one that is attractive because of its glamorous looks or luxuriant coat. It is a no-nonsense kind of a dog that attracts fans on the basis of its capabilities rather than on its beauty points or fad appeal. To its distinct advantage, the Australian cattle dog is not one that registers high on popularity polls, and suitable homes are few and far between. Even those individuals who are attracted to your cattle dog because of its intelligence and protectiveness may not be capable of providing the care and training that made your dog the stellar companion that it is.

While you might never consider allowing your cattle dog to roam the streets or end up in an animal shelter, can you be so sure that someone you sell a puppy to might not do exactly that? As hard as it may be to believe, the Australian Cattle Dog Club of America Rescue Committee is constantly being alerted to Australian cattle dogs that have found their way into animal shelters across America. Many of the rescued animals were born into good homes but obviously fell into the hands of irresponsible buyers.

Suitability as Breeding Stock

Another factor to consider is the suitability of your female, or for that matter your male, for breeding. As previously discussed, not all Australian cattle dogs, even though well-bred, are suitable as breeding stock. If you expressed your future desire to breed Australian cattle dogs with the person from whom you purchased your first dog, the breeder will have undoubtedly selected a pup for you that was worthy of perpetuating the breed. The operative word here of course is "worthy." Your cattle dog may be courageous and protective, and love you beyond all reason, but these are not the criteria for its being a good candidate for producing offspring.

Finding the Right Breeder

If the breeder from whom you purchased your Australian cattle dog sold the dog to you as pet quality only, it is most likely he or she had no desire to have it bred and you should respect that experienced person's wishes. If you are unable to get in touch with the breeder, or if you doubt the credentials of the person from whom you purchased your dog, do some research and find a local breeder who has the reputation for producing show-quality Australian cattle dogs. This is the best person to advise you on whether or not your male or female should be bred.

Relieving the Dog's Frustration?

All too often people who have purchased purebred pets will say to me, "Molly needs to have a litter to complete her development" or "Drover needs a girlfriend to relieve his frustration."

I assure you, neither Molly nor Drover needs sex to make their lives complete. Actually, in the case of Drover or any other male, breeding will serve to increase his frustration rather than relieve it.

Consider the Case of the Puppies

Even if your Australian cattle dog is of the quality that warrants reproducing, there are consequences to breeding that must be considered. Molly's litter can easily bring a household's dog population to half a dozen or more overnight. This is no problem for the first few weeks when the puppies spend their lives nursing and sleeping, but the day very quickly arrives when Molly will look at you as if to say, "Well, you wanted puppies—now take care of them!"

All too soon the puppies will not only want liberation from the whelping box, they will want to be with you—*all of the time!* Think back on the difficulty you experienced in housebreaking and training a single Australian cattle dog puppy. Now multiply that by five or six and consider the cleanup involved for so many pups.

Cages are ideal for housebreaking but no young puppy should be contained for more than a few hours.

You must realize the commitment you will have to make to being on hand when weaning time comes. Newly weaned puppies need four meals a day. Will you or a responsible member of the family be on hand to feed morning, noon, evening, and night?

Australian cattle dog puppies develop and grow rapidly. I assure you they will not be content to be shunted off into some corner, nor will putting them out of sight assist in their all too important socialization. Australian cattle dog puppies must have continuous human contact from birth on if they are to achieve their ultimate as companions. Are you willing to give them all the time they need and deserve until you have found a good, responsible home for each puppy in the litter? This may take weeks, sometimes months, after you have already decided it is time for the puppies to be off to their new homes.

Problems with Males

Males that have been used for breeding may have an extremely difficult time keeping themselves from lifting their leg and "marking" their territory. A male's territory will include everything in your home from new drapery to an antique sofa. Then too, breeding seems to awaken the *machismo* instinct in male Australian cattle dogs. Some stud dogs can become a handful when you are trying to keep them from continually proving they are the toughest kid on the block.

Financial Considerations

Some individuals are willing to commit to all of the above in anticipation of financial gain. They multiply the selling price of a hypothetical number of puppies by somewhere in the area of $500 and think, "Wow, what a great source of income!"

Think again! Stop to consider the cost of a stud fee and prenatal veterinary expenses, then add the cost of possible whelping problems, health checks, and the necessary inoculation series for the puppies. These are all significant cost factors that must be taken into consideration and they are the same factors that will put a very large dent in any anticipated profits.

When the Answer Is "Yes"

If what we have written thus far has not discouraged you and you have decided you really want to raise a litter of Australian cattle dogs, you must begin to plan well ahead. Responsible breeding is not a matter of tossing your female into the back seat of your car and heading for the nearest male of the same breed.

A tip worth considering at this point, especially if this is your first litter: A summer litter is infinitely much easier to care for than one born and growing up during seasons when the weather is inclement. It is much easier to fence off a good-sized area outdoors than to find equal space inside the home. Growing Australian cattle dog puppies need space to exercise and stretch those rapidly growing muscles. The freedom to put what we refer to as our "wrecking crews" safely outdoors during the summer months has proven to be a godsend, and the puppies seem to love it as well.

Helpful hint: Think your planning through carefully. Your female will not whelp until approximately two months after she is bred. The puppies will thus spend the first three or four weeks after they are born in their whelping box; it is during the following eight or twelve weeks that you will welcome good weather.

Health Checks

No Australian cattle dog female should ever be bred until you are sure that she has had at least two heat cycles. Prior to this time she is not completely mature mentally or physi-

cally. You must be sure she is in good health and is not a carrier for the breed's hereditary problems. Some tests such as those for hip dysplasia require X-rays. Eye problems are usually diagnosed by specialists in the field. Tests have also been developed to determine deafness. Your veterinarian can assist you in determining whether any hereditary conditions exist.

All dogs—male and female—must be tested for canine brucellosis before being bred. This is one of the few venereal diseases that afflict dogs. It is a bacterial infection transmitted sexually and through a dog's saliva. It is one cause of abortion in females and of male sterility.

These tests for hereditary problems also apply to your male if he is to be used at stud. Again, we urge the owner of a male to consider the consequences of using the dog for breeding, even once.

Approaches to Breeding

There are three different ways of mating purebred animals of any kind. They are referred to as *inbreeding, outcrossing,* and *linebreeding.* The

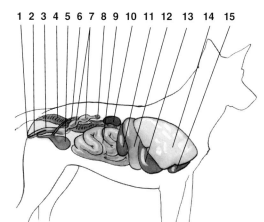

1 2 3 4 5 6 7 8 9 10 11 12 13 14 15

Internal organs of the female Australian cattle dog.

1. vulva
2. vagina
3. cervix
4. descending colon
5. bladder
6. ureter
7. developing embryo
8. ovaries
9. jejunum
10. kidney
11. spleen
12. stomach
13. liver
14. lungs
15. heart

genetic inheritance of the litter your Australian cattle dog female will produce depends upon the relationship of the individuals in her pedigree and the pedigree of the stud dog you eventually select.

Inbreeding

This is an attempt to fix certain mental and physical characteristics in the offspring by mating closely related individuals. Breedings between mother and son, father and daughter, and brother and sister are examples of inbreeding. Inbreeding fixes both qualities and faults; therefore, it is a method that should be resorted to only by experienced Australian cattle dog breeders who are completely familiar with the pedigrees and possible problems in the pedigrees of the two animals involved in the mating.

Outcrossing

Outcrossing is the opposite of inbreeding. This method of breeding mates individuals that, for all intents and purposes, are not related but are of the same breed. This approach is less likely to fix faults in the offspring, but neither can it concentrate specific qualities with any certainty.

Linebreeding

This might be considered the happy medium between inbreeding and outcrossing and is the method by which most quality Australian cattle dogs are produced. Related animals are used but the common ancestor or ancestors may be two or three generations removed. Linebreeding affords the same benefits and drawbacks of inbreeding, but to a lesser degree.

Selecting the Stud Dog

The decision to breed your female was based upon the fact that she is of the quality and temperament that make her a likely candidate to pro-

duce worthy offspring. This does not mean she is a perfect Australian cattle dog by any stretch of the imagination. No dog of any breed is perfect—not even the greatest show winner. The likelihood of your female Australian cattle dog having no faults to compensate for in selecting a stud dog is extremely remote. The stud dog you select should excel in those areas in which your female has shortcomings, but above all he must have a sound and stable temperament. Responsible Australian cattle dog breeders must never settle for anything less.

As you read through the American Kennel Club's standard of perfection for the Australian cattle dog (see pages 13–15) you may be able to note areas in which your female does not quite measure up; however, this is an extremely difficult judgment for a novice to make, and it is here that the breeder from whom you purchased your Australian cattle dog is invaluable. Experienced breeders have studied long and hard to learn which males and females are best suited for breeding and will advise accordingly.

The Australian cattle dog male advertised in the newspaper or owned by an acquaintance may carry none of the compensating qualities your female needs in her offspring. Worse, an irresponsibly chosen mate for your female might conceivably carry faults in his genetic makeup that, added to those in your female's genes, will create serious problems in the next generation. For instance, doubling up on the genes that produce unreliable temperament may produce aggressive, uncontrollable offspring even though the male and female used appear to be sound and stable.

The breeder of your female will be familiar with the pedigree, conformation, and temperament—all the assets and the shortcomings of the line of Australian cattle dogs from which your female descends. Your breeder will also be the best person to advise you on which faults your female has that the proper stud dog should be able to compensate for.

If the breeder of your female is not available for some reason, the Australian Cattle Dog Club of America maintains a list of responsible breeders. You may be able to select someone who lives nearby who can offer sound advice regarding the proper selection of a stud dog.

Agreements between Owners

Paperwork

The owner of a stud dog should be able to present proof that care and testing indicates the stud dog is not a carrier of the hereditary problems of the breed. You should be able to provide proof of your female's health as well.

The stud dog owner will be able to provide you with a four-generation pedigree of his or her dog. You should also bring a copy of your female's pedigree when you first go to see the stud dog. The owner of the stud will be anxious to see if your female's bloodlines will be compatible with those of the stud. You can also ask the owner of the stud how to go about arranging to have the forthcoming litter registered.

Stud Fee

The cost of breeding to the male you select (the stud fee) should be determined in advance as well. Stud fees vary depending upon the male's proven ability to produce quality puppies. The cost of breeding to a young male that has yet to produce a litter is going to be much less than that of a male that has produced many champion offspring. The predictability of what kind of offspring the unproven male will be able to produce is also significantly less. Again, you get what

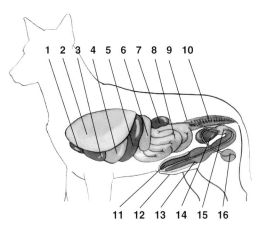

1. thymus
2. lung
3. heart
4. liver
5. stomach
6. spleen
7. kidney
8. jejunum
9. ureter
10. descending colon
11. penis
12. penis sheath
13. penis bulb
14. bladder
15. prostrate
16. testes

Internal organs of the male Australian cattle dog.

you pay for. Since it is unlikely that you will breed many Australian cattle dog litters in your lifetime, why not attempt to breed the very best possible litter and thus make a genuine contribution to the breed that you obviously enjoy?

The stud fee is always payable at the time of breeding and is payment for breeding your female to the designated male—nothing more; it is not a guarantee of living puppies. Most cattle dog breeders will give a return service as a courtesy should the female not become pregnant, but that should definitely be discussed and put in writing if the stud dog owner is agreeable to providing this return service.

Breeding Agreement

Any agreements and conditions outside of a guarantee of actual mating should be clearly outlined in a stud contract or breeding agreement. This agreement should list the amount of the stud fee and any special conditions that apply. If the female is to remain on the premises of the stud owner while she is being bred, the contract should also state what additional costs are

A conscientious breeder will be committed to assuring that each and every puppy will be well-cared for.

Breeding Reservation

Once the stud dog has been decided upon, the owner of the female should make a breeding reservation based upon the regularity of the female's previous seasons. This will give the owner of a popular stud dog the opportunity to schedule other females that may be coming in to breed to the dog of your choice.

When the Female Is "In Heat"

The female can be bred only at a particular time during her heat cycle, which lasts approximately 21 days. Most females will normally come into heat, called *estrus*, for the first time at about ten to twelve months of age; it can take place as early as six months. After her first heat, your female will be in heat again fairly regularly every six to eight months thereafter.

A noticeable swelling of the vulva, accompanied by a dark bloody vaginal discharge, is the first sign that your female is in heat. Once you have noticed this, she should be watched very carefully and kept away from all males to avoid any accidental matings. She should also be confined to an area of the household where the discharge, which she is unable to control, will not soil carpeting or furniture.

If your female is to be bred at this season, you should at once notify the owner of the stud dog you have chosen. The owner of the stud dog can then schedule the breeding and tell you when to arrive with your female.

I cannot caution you enough to be extremely watchful while your female is in heat. You cannot imagine how many unwanted litters have been born even though the female was, "only with a male too young (or too old) to breed," or "in the yard by herself just a few minutes." You would be amazed at how innovative the ready

involved in keeping her there. The contract should state what the owner of the stud dog is responsible for while the female is in residence.

Pick of the Litter

On occasion, the owner of an Australian cattle dog stud dog will agree to have his or her dog mate your female in return for first choice of the resulting puppies. This can be a good arrangement for someone who does not plan on keeping a puppy from the litter for themselves. If the owner of the female plans to keep a pup from the litter to show or to breed or for any other reason, this option should be considered carefully. It is extremely difficult to give up the puppy you had grown attached to or planned to keep as a show prospect, even when you have agreed to do so beforehand. More often than not, the breeder of the litter and the stud dog owner wind up wanting the same puppy.

Australian cattle dog female and the always ready male can be when the time is right!

It is commonly accepted that females of almost all breeds are not ready to accept the male until about the tenth day of their heat cycle. Do not, however, allow that information lull you into believing that your Australian cattle dog *cannot* be bred before or after that time. While desired matings seldom are accomplished prior to the tenth day of the heat cycle, it seems *unwanted* matings are productive at almost any time the female is in heat. As a rule, however, most Australian cattle dog females are ready to breed later in their season rather than earlier.

Timing Is Critical

A veterinarian can be extremely helpful in advising the right day on which to breed your female. Blood tests and vaginal smears can be performed that will determine just when the female's ovulation has begun and the right time to have her bred. At this time she releases eggs that must be fertilized by the dog's sperm for pregnancy to occur. Experienced breeders, and very often, experienced stud dogs have an uncanny knack of being able to determine the correct day on which a female should be bred.

Even when ovulation has occurred, it may take hours or even a couple of days before the eggs are receptive to sperm. Because of the gradual ovulation, even after the first successful mating has been completed, it is wise to repeat the breeding again once or twice, skipping a day between breedings to insure pregnancy.

Even though your female has been successfully mated to the dog of your choice, do not assume she cannot be impregnated by another dog. She must be closely watched until she has completely ended her heat cycle. Litters can be produced that have had two or more entirely different sires, one a purebred Australian cattle dog, the other a dog of mixed parentage or of another breed. None of the puppies born from a litter of this kind may be registered, as they are all of doubtful parentage, but this does not mean that your female is "tainted" for life. Her subsequent litters will not be affected in any way if she is properly mated and watched.

Pregnancy, Whelping, and Raising Puppies

Is She Or Isn't She?

There is nothing radically different you need do for your female Australian cattle dog for the first four or five weeks after she has been bred; maintain her normal schedule and diet. There is no reason to restrict the amount of exercise she has been used to. In fact, maintaining good muscle tone will serve her well when whelping actually occurs.

We know we cannot tell if one of our females has become pregnant for several weeks after she has been bred. Still, we invariably lapse into what we call our staring mode. While caught up in this phase we gaze intently at the mother-to-be, noting any little sign that will indicate that she is or is not pregnant. We change our minds daily, sometimes hourly, but in the end we must wait about five weeks when a swelling of the female's nipples will indicate that the breeding has apparently taken.

Preparations

The Whelping Box

The gestation period is normally 59 to 63 days, which gives you plenty of time to be well prepared for the birth of the litter. One of the first orders of business should be preparing a whelping box where mother and offspring will spend the first several weeks of their life together.

The whelping box can be made from a cardboard shipping carton or constructed of wood. Our suggestion would be to purchase or build a box constructed of wood as the puppies will continue to use it as their bed even after they have been weaned. As the puppies grow, you will find them leaving the whelping box to relieve themselves, thus assisting you in the first stages of their housebreaking.

The box should be approximately 48 inches (122 cm) square with sides about 10 inches (25 cm) high. The box need not be covered, but if it is, the top should be high enough to allow the mother to stand upright and at least one side should be low enough to allow the female easy access. Whelping boxes of various shapes and sizes can be obtained at most pet stores, or if carpentry is your long suit, a whelping box can easily

The mother cattle dog and her offspring will spend the first several weeks of their life together in the whelping box.

be constructed of inexpensive, well-sanded wood.

The important thing is that your female should be able to hop in and out of the whelping box easily without injuring her puppies. Once in, she should be able to stretch out fully on her side so that all of her nipples will be available for the puppies to nurse on. Keep the bottom of the whelping box lined with several layers of newspaper or unprinted newspaper stock that can be obtained at most printing shops and will keep mother and puppies much cleaner looking.

Prenatal Care

As previously mentioned, there is little different that must be done for the first several weeks of pregnancy. If the female has been fed a nutritious, well-balanced diet, you need only continue doing so.

At about the fifth week of her pregnancy her appetite will increase and you may begin to add to the amount of food she is receiving. Do not overfeed, and do not feel she must be given special food or treats; you should avoid allowing the pregnant female to become too fat as obesity can create serious problems at whelping time. Since the female's abdomen is already crowded, several smaller meals during the course of the day will be more beneficial than allowing her to gorge herself once or twice a day.

Some dog owners feel that megadoses of vitamins are necessary during pregnancy. This is definitely not so. In fact, many experienced breeders now feel that large doses of vitamins are dangerous because, improperly administered, there can be long-range detrimental effects on a dog's skeletal development. It must be remembered that the vast majority of commercial dog foods are highly fortified to begin with, so adding high concentrations of additional vitamins

Standby Whelping Equipment
- whelping box
- newsprint or newspaper
- toweling
- gauze pads
- small box with adjustable heating pad
- emergency supplemental feeder
- mother's milk replacement
- glucose
- rectal thermometer
- disposable rubber gloves
- blunt sterilized scissors
- cotton thread
- lubricant
- scale
- infrared lamp
- telephone numbers: Veterinarian's or 24-hour emergency clinics
- patience!

without careful consideration can create problems.

Your veterinarian can advise you when and if any vitamins or medications are necessary. Veterinarians should also be told of your female's pregnancy prior to treatment of any kind, as no inoculations should be given that will affect the normal growth of the fetuses she is carrying.

Whelping the Litter

As the time draws near for the actual whelping, it is wise to assemble the items that will assist you in insuring that the delivery will go smoothly.

Ordinarily, whelping an Australian cattle dog litter progresses with few complications. The breed is basically healthy with none of the abnormal breed points that make whelping difficult in some other breeds. Most Australian cattle dog females whelp their own puppies naturally with little assistance from their owner.

Even first-time mothers sever the umbilical cord and clean the puppies

The birth sequence: 1. The puppy is expelled in the birth sac. 2. The mother clears the sac away from face and eats the after-birth (placenta). 3. Puppy's anogenial regions are licked. 4. Puppies nurse.

without any assistance. The owner's only duty is to stand by with a watchful eye just in case complications arise.

Whelping a litter for the first time usually proves to be more traumatic for the owner than for the dog. Mother Nature has provided your cattle dog with a whole set of instinctive behaviors that will take place when the proper time comes. On the very rare occasion that your female does not respond properly or that you suspect something is wrong, call your veterinarian. A veterinarian is trained to know what to do and when to do it. Why should you try to guess your way along when years of study and experience are as accessible as your telephone?

When the Female Starts to Whelp

It is wise to be completely prepared for the female to start whelping at least a week before the time she is actually due. Some females are a few days early, others a few days late. If one of our females is running late we usually take her to our veterinarian just to make sure there are no complications. We have had an occasional female whelp as much as a week late with no difficulties, but, it is better to be safe than sorry.

This is not the time to allow your female to be outdoors alone for more than a few minutes. You cannot imagine how inventive some Australian cattle dog mothers-to-be can become in finding a little den under the house or some other inaccessible place to whelp her puppies. It can and does happen. Keep her in or near her whelping box as much as possible.

The female's temperature will usually drop from a normal of 101.5°F (38.6°C) to 99°F (37.2°C) within 48 hours of the time she will begin whelping. This is often accompanied by general restlessness, shivering, and panting.

There will often be a clear mucous discharge from the vulva that will act as a lubricant during the whelping process. The female will begin scratching in her whelping box, preparing a "nest" in which to deposit her puppies. Some females will vomit during this stage.

These signs can continue for up to 24 hours before contractions actually commence. Although it is obvious the female is experiencing discomfort, there is no need to be unduly concerned unless she appears to be in pain.

Uterine contractions increase in frequency and intensity and the vulva and vagina slowly begin to dilate. Often, the laboring mother will swing around to investigate her rear end and then lie down, stretching her rear legs to press against the sides of the whelping box or squat and strain as if she is trying to relieve her bowels. She may howl or whimper during these contractions.

If contractions continue and no puppies arrive during the next two hours you should definitely seek the advice of your veterinarian. In some cases a puppy is too large to be passed naturally and a cesarean section may be needed.

The First Puppy Arrives

The first puppy is usually preceded by a water bag that breaks and serves as a warning that a puppy is about to be whelped. After a few minutes and more contractions, the first puppy will work its way along the birth canal and begin to emerge from the vulva, usually head first. Once the head has emerged, the female may rest a moment or two before expelling the rest of the whelp. It will be contained in a membrane sac sometimes connected by the umbilical cord, to the placenta.

The puppy must be removed from the sac either by the mother or by you. Normally, the mother immediately gets to work and does all that is necessary, breaking open the sac, biting through the umbilical cord, and licking the puppy until it gives out a loud cry.

If There Is a Problem with a Puppy

On a rare occasion, a female whelping her first litter may seem to be

If the mother does not remove the birth-sac it is time to act. Break open the membrane at the puppy's head and grasp the umbilical cord about two inches (5 cm) from the abdomen.

totally surprised by the arrival of her first puppy and, lacking the maternal instinct, will only look at it in amazement. It is then time for you to act. If the puppy remains in the sac it will drown and die.

Break open the membrane at the puppy's head and grasp the umbilical cord about two inches (5 cm) from the abdomen, draining the fluid in the cord toward the puppy. Immediately sever the cord at this point with the sterilized scissors.

Rub the puppy vigorously with rough toweling to stimulate circulation. It is wise to make sure that the puppy's nose and throat are clear of mucus at this time. Support the puppy in the palm of one hand with its head toward your fingers. Cover and hold the puppy securely with your other hand. Raise your arms above your head and swing the puppy downward in an arc. The centrifugal force will expel any fluids remaining in the nasal or throat passages. Newborn puppies are far less fragile than most people imagine, so do not be afraid to be vigorous in stimulating the newborn whelp. Use a drop of disinfectant to

To expel all fluids from a puppy's lungs support the puppy between the palms of the hands and raising your arms above your head, swing the puppy downward in an arc.

sterilize the cut end of the umbilical cord still attached to the puppy.

If the placenta has not been expelled along with the puppy, the female will normally do so shortly after the puppy is born. There is one placenta for every puppy born and they must each be accounted for. The mother instinctively wants to eat the placentas and we allow her to have one, because the placenta contains useful nutrients. However, allowing her to eat them all can lead to severe diarrhea, so we quickly remove the rest as they are passed, wrap them in newspaper, and place them in the trash.

Breech Births

Barring unforeseen circumstances, the puppies will usually follow each other in irregular succession. Australian cattle dog litters can vary in number from three to four or as high as eight to nine puppies. There is no need to be concerned if the female takes time out to rest between births. If she continues to strain and no puppies are passed, consult your veterinarian.

Normally, puppies are born head first, but there is an occasional breech birth in which the puppy is born hind legs first. There is no real need to worry about this, because as we previously stated there are no structural exaggerations in the Australian cattle dog that in themselves would lead to difficult whelping. Breech births in large-headed breeds like bulldogs, Boston terriers, etc. can be difficult, because the head of the puppy may not be easily passed.

We gently assist breech births if it appears necessary, and especially if the breech occurs further along in the whelping process. At this point, the female may be tired and the contractions not as strong. In this case, all that needs to be done is to firmly grasp as much of the portion of the puppy that has emerged. As the contractions occur, simultaneously ease the puppy out. It is important to have a firm grasp on as much of the puppy's body as possible when you do this. Do not pull sharply, as you risk injuring the mother. Should you be unable to dislodge the puppy in this manner after ten to fifteen minutes, consult your veterinarian.

After Whelping

Dinner Time

Once a puppy has been dried and we are sure it is breathing properly, we allow it to nurse on the mother until contractions begin again. Among the many things with which Mother Nature has endowed the Australian cattle dog, the will to survive is extremely high on the list. You will be amazed at the vigor of the newborn Australian cattle dog whelps and how quickly they find their mother's milk bar and commence nursing. It is only the rare cattle dog puppy that needs to be guided to its mother's nipple or given assistance to nurse. More often than not it is a case of insuring that the larger, stronger puppies do not push their smaller littermates out of the way and keep them from getting their fair share of milk.

When the mother's birth contractions resume, we remove the previously born puppies and place them in a small box right next to the whelping box so the female can see that her puppies are safe as she prepares to give birth to the next one. On the bottom of the small box we place a not-too-hot water bottle covered in towels. This will keep the puppies warm while they are away from the mother. It is crucial that newborn and nursing puppies not become chilled, as their temperature-regulating systems are not fully functional at this stage.

We keep water available for the female and also a bowl of broth or milk kept at room temperature throughout the whelping process. Once whelping has been completed and we have cleaned up the whelping box, we offer the nursing mother light

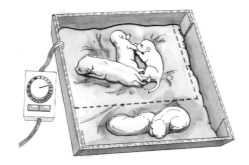

When the mother's birth contractions resume, remove the previously born puppies and place them in a small box so the female can see her puppies are safe. Place a hot water bottle or heating pad, covered by a towel, on the bottom of the box.

food, such as chicken and rice or even scrambled eggs.

Veterinary Checkup

Retaining a placenta can cause serious infection. If you suspect one has been retained, mention this to your veterinarian when you take the mother and puppies in for their first checkup. It is wise to have this checkup performed within 24 hours of whelping to avoid any complications and to make sure the mother has not retained any puppies. The veterinarian will also inspect the puppies at this time to make sure there are no abnormalities.

Peace and Quiet

Other than the important trip to the veterinarian, the mother and puppies should be given as much peace and quiet as possible. Undoubtedly, everyone in the household, if not the entire neighborhood, will want to see the puppies, but the mother wants and deserves privacy. Mother Australian cattle dogs are very protective of their offspring and strangers coming and going can be upsetting. It is not

The vigor of newborn Australian cattle dog whelps is amazing. The puppies quickly find their mother's milk bar and commence nursing.

Post-whelping Complications

Australian cattle dog mothers are not generally prone to post-whelping complications, but occasionally problems do develop. It is important to be aware of the symptoms to avoid serious complications.

Mastitis: An inflammation of the mammary glands usually associated with bacterial infections, the infection is introduced via the bloodstream through a skin lesion or through the teat canal. An excess of milk in the female can also cause the breasts to become hard and painful. This is common when nursing females have only one or two puppies and too much milk, with some nipples hardly used. Examine breasts regularly and massage them gently if milk is building up. If your female seems to be in pain or if one or more glands seem excessively red or hot to the touch, call your veterinarian at once.

Eclampsia: This is a much more serious condition but far less common than mastitis. It is caused by a shortage of calcium in the bloodstream. It may occur just before or any time after whelping, but usually at about three to four weeks after the puppies are born. Symptoms are the mother's extreme restlessness, often along with shivering and vomiting. Her legs or entire body can go stiff, and convulsions may occur. Veterinary treatment must be sought at once. Massive injections of calcium are usually administered and recovery is normally rapid, but the mother should not be returned to her litter, as she will undoubtedly relapse.

Metritis: Metritis is an inflammation of the uterus, and is usually the result of contamination entering the uterus during whelping, or from a retained placenta, or sometimes as a result of bacterial contamination during mating. Fever, abdominal pain, discharge from the vulva, and straining may be seen.

beyond an otherwise calm and friendly cattle dog mother to greet people she does not know well with a threatening growl at this time.

What the new mother needs is privacy, and allowing her this opportunity will permit her to settle in with the important duties of motherhood. Warmth and sustenance are primarily what young puppies require. A constant flow of strangers upsets the mother and disturbs the puppies.

Water and Food

Make sure the mother has plenty to drink at all times from this point on. She must not become dehydrated.

The female's appetite will begin to increase significantly within a day or two and she should be fed several times a day, giving her as much as she wants to eat. Her regular nourishing meals should be resumed and supplemented with meaty soups and thick broths. We usually switch to puppy chow in place of the regular adult kibble, because there are more nutrients in these special formulas.

Although raising a litter of cattle dog puppies involves a great deal of care and commitment, responsible owners can take pride in producing sound, healthy puppies that will be capable of being outstanding companions.

Veterinary care is essential to treat this condition.

Pyometra: Pyometra is not directly related to the birth process but occurs between heat periods. Bacteria in the resting uterus multiply and the resulting infection fills the uterus with pus. The bitch often exhibits depression, a fever, and there may be a bloody or foul-smelling discharge from the vulva. In some cases there may be no discharge, but the uterus may be swollen and the abdomen tender. Advanced cases are very serious and may be life-threatening. This condition can be treated only by a veterinarian, and surgery may be necessary

Caring for the Puppies

Hand-rearing

It is a rare situation in which an Australian cattle dog mother cannot take care of her own puppies, but sometimes a puppy or an entire litter will have to be given supplemental feedings or be completely hand-raised. There are a number of reasons that this may be necessary. At times, there are individual puppies in the litter that are too weak to obtain the necessary amount of milk to maintain optimum growth, or the mother may not be able to nurse any of her puppies because of complications of one sort or another.

Warmth and regular feedings every two hours are critical here. A constant temperature of 85°F (29°C) can be controlled with an infrared lamp suspended above the whelping box.

We keep mother's milk replacement and all the necessary feeding apparatus on hand prior to whelping day, just in case assistance must be given. Veterinarians are probably the best source of these items and you can get necessary instructions in how to hand-feed should you have to do so.

It is very important to follow all instructions from your veterinarian and

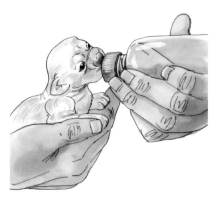

Sometimes a puppy or an entire litter will need supplemental feedings or be completely hand-raised. Average-size newborn Australian cattle dog puppies can be fed with a human baby's bottle with a baby-sized nipple.

those on the feeding product container. A puppy's digestive system is very delicate and can easily be upset, causing diarrhea, dehydration, and even death.

There are many different methods used by breeders and recommended by veterinarians that can be used for supplemental feeding. Discuss this issue with your veterinarian, who can not only provide you with any equipment you might need, but also give you instructions on how to properly proceed with hand-rearing or supplementing for a puppy or the entire litter.

Bottle-feeding

For average-size newborn Australian cattle dog puppies, use a human baby's bottle with a baby-sized nipple for hand-feeding. The puppies will learn to use these nipples quite easily. Puppies that nurse naturally on their mother suck far more than just the nipple itself into their mouths; therefore, they have little or no trouble using the baby bottle method.

Place the puppy on a rough bath towel on your lap. This surface allows the puppy to dig in with its hindquar-

ters and gain traction, enabling it to "knead" with its front legs while it is nursing. We find using this method most closely approximates natural nursing and has been the most successful, causing the fewest problems in the long run.

The puppy may not accept the nipple at first and you may have to gently open its mouth. Make sure the puppy's tongue is at the bottom of the mouth so that it can suck properly. It will be easier to insert the nipple into the puppy's mouth if the nipple is squeezed flat.

If the puppy does not start sucking immediately, squeeze a few drops of milk into its mouth. Usually a taste of what is yet to come will inspire most puppies to start sucking in earnest. Still, there is the reluctant pup who is bound and determined that Mom is the only way to go, and you will have to be a bit more persistent and patient. Be sure to keep the bottle tilted at an angle so that the nipple is continually filled with milk, as you do not want the puppy to suck in air.

Newborn puppies need small quantities, often. They will usually pull back and turn their heads when satisfied. As long as their abdomens seem firm and filled, but not bloated, they are doing just fine. If a puppy seems gaunt and is not gaining weight, consult your veterinarian.

If you are completely taking over for the puppies' mother you will have to perform the functions the mother normally assumes. Clean the puppies mouth of any milk that has accumulated there with a piece of cotton slightly dampened with warm water. Using another swap, gently rub around the area from which the puppy urinates to stimulate it to pass water. This also must be done under the abdomen and around the anal region, encouraging the puppy to empty its bowels.

When this has been accomplished, rub these same areas with a very small amount of Vaseline to avoid chafing and irritation. This procedure must be repeated every time the puppies are bottle-fed.

Obviously, this procedure is going to take a significant amount of time. Hand-rearing puppies is no mean feat, especially during the first two weeks when the newborn whelps must be fed every two hours. After the second week, feeding times may be spaced to two-and-a-half to three hours apart. By the end of the third week, you can begin introducing the orphans to solid food.

Using Caution

Puppies that have been nursing on their mother's milk will have derived a natural immunity from her that will last several weeks and after which they will need individual immunization. Puppies that have been completely hand-raised will not have this immunity and must be protected from coming in contact with any of the airborne contagious diseases. These can be carried on the hands and shoes of almost anyone, so it is imperative to keep the puppy area as sterile as possible. Have any visiting strangers remove their shoes before entering the puppy room. We find it best not to have strangers handle the puppies at all until after the initial inoculations have been given.

Weaning

At about ten days old, most puppies' eyes will have begun to open; once all of the puppies in the litter have their eyes open, weaning can commence. If the litter has been nursing on their mother, weaning does not necessarily have to take place this early, but at this point even the most diligent mother begins to spend progressively more time away from her puppies—her little angels are rapidly developing needlelike teeth and can be quite tyrannical in having their needs met.

As this happens, it is time for you to step in and offer a hand. The easiest way to assist the transition of puppies from entire dependency upon their mother to a self-sufficient state is to allow the transition to happen gradually.

Puppy chows: There are now good-quality puppy chows available that can be soaked and made into an easily digestible mixture from the first day of weaning. You can use cow's milk, goat's milk, or any one of a number of commercial brands prepared especially for dogs.

Mother should have some outdoor time while you are feeding her puppies or she will eat what you have put down and then regurgitate the food for the puppies. This is a natural instinct of canine mothers as their offspring come toward the end of their nursing phase and are ready to eat on their own.

It is not unusual to see a nursing mother regurgitate her own food for her puppies, especially if she is fed and then allowed to immediately return to the puppies. Most humans find this a disturbing and offensive habit, but it is not harmful to the puppies in any way unless the mother has passed back large lumps of meat or other solid food. To avoid this, it is best to keep the mother away from her puppies for at least an hour after she has eaten.

Raising the Litter

Once the puppies are completely weaned, they should learn to eat from separate dishes. It is not unusual to have one or two bullies in the litter who stand in the communal food pan and intimidate a more reticent littermate. Separate dishes will allow you to see how much each puppy is eating and to feed the slow eater alone, if necessary.

A healthy puppy is a delight for everyone in the home.

should be semisolid food and the other one or two meals can consist of milk with perhaps a small amount of baby cereal or puppy kibble added.

Australian cattle dog puppies need to be treated for roundworms beginning at three or four weeks of age. Your veterinarian will prescribe the proper treatment and the frequency of subsequent wormings.

We try to keep strangers away from the puppies as much as possible until the puppies have had their initial inoculations. On the other hand, we encourage every member of the household to handle each puppy regularly. We have always maintained the best place for the puppy playpen is in the kitchen, where there is constant traffic and all kinds of odd noises. If there are children in the household, teach them how to play with the puppies gently. All these things will add up to a well-socialized puppy, ready to go off to its new owners and provide them with years of friendship and entertainment.

You will have done your job well.

The puppies should be fed four times a day starting first thing in the morning and about every four to five hours thereafter. At least three of these meals

Useful Addresses and Literature

Kennel Clubs and Organizations

American Herding Breed Association
Linda C. Rorem
1548 Victoria Road
Pacifica, CA 94044

American Kennel Club
51 Madison Avenue
New York, NY 10010
(212) 696-8200

All Registration Information:
American Kennel Club
5580 Centerview Drive
Raleigh, NC 27606
(919) 233-9767

Australian Cattle Dog Club of America
91 Sun Valley Road
Tularosa, NM 88352

Australian Cattle Dog Club of America
Rescue League
John Krupas
(313) 366-0537 (Michigan)

Australian National Kennel Council
Royal Showgrounds
Ascot Vale 3032
Victoria, Australia

Canadian Kennel Club
89 Skyway Avenue, Unit 100
Etobicoke, Ontario
Canada M9W 6R4
(416) 675-5511

The Kennel Club
1-5 Clargis Street
Piccadilly, London W1Y 8AB
England

New Zealand Kennel Club
Private Bag 59003
Porirua, Wellington
New Zealand

United Kennel Club
100 E. Kilgore Road
Kalamazoo, MI 49001-5598

United Schutzhund Clubs of America
c/o Paul Meloy
3704 Lemay Ferry Road
St. Louis, MO 63125

United States Dog Agility Association
P.O. Box 850955
Richardson, TX 75085-0955

The Australian cattle dog is a curious, innovative companion.

Books

Colflesh, Linda. *Making Friends*. New York: Howell Book House, 1990.

De Prisco, Andrew and Johnson, James B. *Canine Lexicon*. Neptune City, New Jersey: T.F.H. Publications, Inc., 1993.

Fiennes, Alice and Richard. *The Natural History of Dogs*. Garden City, New York: The Natural History Press, 1970.

Fox, Dr. Michael W. *Superdog*. New York: Howell Book House, 1990.

Harling, Donn and Deborah. *Australian Cattle Dogs (The First Five Years)*. Topeka, Kansas: Donn and Deborah Harling, 1986.

Holmes, John and Mary. *The Complete Australian Cattle Dog*. New York: Howell Book House, Macmillan Publishing Company, 1993.

Shaffer, Mari. *Heeler Power*. Waterloo, Wisconsin: Countryside Publications, Ltd. 1984.

Squire, Dr. Ann. *Understanding Man's Best Friend*. New York: Macmillan Publishing Company, 1991.

Periodicals

AKC Gazette
51 Madison Avenue
New York, NY 10010

Bloodlines
United Kennel Club
100 E. Kilgore Road
Kalamazoo, MI 49001-5598

Dog Fancy
P.O. Box 6050
Mission Viejo, CA 92690
(800) 426-2516

Dog World
29 North Wacker Drive
Chicago, IL 60606
(312) 726-2802

Dogs In Canada
Apex Publishers
89 Skyway Ave.#200
Etobicoke, Ontario
Canada M9W-6R4

National Stockdog Magazine
P.O. Box 402
3597 CR 75
Butler, IN
(219) 868-2670

Index